Chef Paul Prudhomme's

LOUISIANA CAJUN MAGIC®

Cookbook

PUBLICATIONS
INTERNATIONAL, LTD.

Contents

All photography by Will Crocker.

Library of Congress Catalog Card Number: 89-61433

ISBN: 0-88176-675-5

PUBLICATIONS INTERNATIONAL, LTD.

This edition published by:
Publications International, Ltd.
7373 N. Cicero
Lincolnwood, IL 60646

Pictured on the front cover: Chef Paul Prudhomme holding Velvet Shrimp with pasta (*see page 68*).

Pictured on the back cover (on the left, top to bottom): Omelette Jardinier (*see page 88*), Chicken, Andouille Smoked Sausage and Tasso Jambalaya (*see page 58*) and Island Chicken Salad with Brilliant Spice Dressing (*see page 16*). On the right: Low-Calorie Seafood Okra Gumbo (*see page 20*).

If you would like more information about Cajun Magic® seasoning, call 1-800-4-K-PAULS (outside Louisiana) or 504-947-6712 (in Louisiana) or write to K-Paul's Louisiana Enterprises, Post Office Box 770034, New Orleans, LA 70177-0034.

h g f e d c b a

Manufactured in Yugoslavia

Cooking with Cajun Magic

Hello, my name is Paul Prudhomme and I'd like to talk to you a minute and tell you about this book that you're holding in your hand. When I was first approached with the idea of doing this CAJUN MAGIC® book, I saw it as an exciting opportunity to quickly reach thousands of you who would not ordinarily have a chance to experience what a difference CAJUN MAGIC® herb and spice blends will make in your everyday cooking.

Most of the world thinks of Louisiana food as very hot, but that's not true! Louisiana cooking really is creating wonderful tasting food using fresh, locally available ingredients. The difference in the food comes from a Cajun/Creole tradition of a people who pride themselves in their ability to make food taste different, exciting and good!

One of the keys to Louisiana cooking is the consistent use of herbs and spices to build and improve on the food's flavor. We use an array of seasonings that caress your taste buds without overpowering them. There is nothing magical about the cooking methods. It's the blending of herbs and spices in just the right combination that is the secret.

After trying several of my recipes, take one of your family favorites and apply what you've learned about our cooking methods and seasonings. You'll be pleased at the exciting, new sensations in taste and smell that you'll discover. Try something "new" once or twice a week and enjoy the results. You'll get tremendous satisfaction from your efforts and the pleasure expressed by family and friends.

For every meal that you fix, you can find tips in this book that will help you fix that meal better. And probably the most important tip is using CAJUN MAGIC®—the seasoning blends used in the wide variety of recipes I have developed for you in the following pages.

The convenience and simplicity of having a complete seasoning blend is truly magical. I discovered this important fact a long time ago and cannot overemphasize what a difference a quality seasoning blend will make in your cooking.

Pick a dish from this book that fits your taste, mood or life-style. We offer recipes that are quick and easy, some that are great for use as leftovers and others that are more traditional and take a little longer to prepare. Whether you're fixing something for breakfast, lunch, dinner or a snack, we want you to understand that you can use CAJUN MAGIC® every day to make your life in the kitchen simpler and more exciting. It makes your seasoning decisions easy—all the blends are designed to be complete—just add them as you would salt and pepper.

What greater pleasure is there in life than cooking something exciting to eat for someone you love. To watch someone's eyes light up and know that you created something that gave them great pleasure—that's what CAJUN MAGIC® is all about—giving an emotional excitement to food.

Preparation Techniques

1.

2.

3.

4.

Forming a Crust on Bottom of Skillet

1. Ingredients are added to a heavy skillet.

2. Cook until the bottom of the skillet is covered with browned bits. At this point, flour can be added.

3. Continue cooking, stirring, until the flour mixture is rich brown and has formed a thin crust in the bottom of the skillet.

4. Slowly stir in liquid, stirring and scraping skillet bottom to remove all browned bits. This is called deglazing and the result is a wonderful gravy.

1.

2.

Caramelizing Onions

1. Chopped onions are cooked in hot oil until softened and beginning to brown. Seasonings are added.

2. Reduce heat and cook onions, stirring frequently, until onions are caramelized (a rich brown color) but not burned.

1.

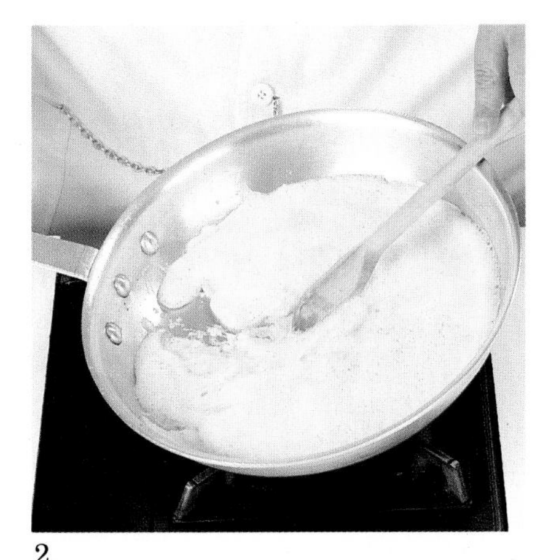

2.

Making Omelets

1. As soon as there is a base of cooked egg on the bottom of the skillet, pull eggs from outside of pan toward the middle.

2. Continue pulling cooked portion toward center of pan until eggs are almost cooked through but top is still loose.

1.

2.

Making a Roux

1. In large heavy skillet, heat oil to smoking. Using a *long*-handled metal whisk or wooden spoon, gradually stir in flour, whisking constantly. (If black specks appear in the roux as it cooks, it has burned and cannot be used. If you feel it's getting away from you, remove it from the heat until you have control of it.) Continue whisking until roux reaches the desired color (medium-brown shown here). Immediately remove from heat to stop the cooking process.

2. This roux has been taken to a dark red-brown. Its flavor is somewhat stronger, deeper and nuttier. Traditionally a light roux is used with dark meats such as beef and duck. A dark roux is used with sweet, light meats such as pork, rabbit and veal, and also with fish and shellfish. And a black roux is best for gumbo. You can experiment with endless combinations of roux colors and your ingredients to arrive at the tastes that excite you most!

1.

2.

Making Chicken or Meat Stock

1. Meat or chicken pieces used for stock should first be roasted in the oven until very brown. Then combine them with the vegetables and cold water in a stockpot.

2. Strain stock before using.

Great for the Grill

Magic Grilled Fish

Whether you have a charcoal or gas grill, prepare the hottest fire possible.

6 (1/2-inch-thick) firm-fleshed fish fillets (8 to 10 ounces each), such as redfish, pompano, tilefish, red snapper, or salmon or tuna steaks
3/4 cup (1 1/2 sticks) unsalted butter, melted
3 tablespoons plus 2 teaspoons CAJUN MAGIC Blackened Redfish Magic®

Heat grill as hot as possible and have flames reaching above grates before putting fish on grill. Add dry wood chunks to glowing coals to make the fire hotter.

Dip each fillet in melted butter so that both sides are well coated, then sprinkle Blackened Redfish Magic generously and evenly on both sides of fillets, patting it in by hand. Place fillets directly over flame on very hot grill and pour 1 teaspoon of the melted butter on top of each. (Be careful; butter may flare up.) Cook, uncovered, directly in flames until underside looks blackened, about 2 minutes. (Time will vary according to each fillet's thickness and heat of grill.) Turn fish over and grill until cooked through, about 2 minutes more. Serve piping hot with assorted grilled vegetables.

Makes 6 servings

Magic Grilled Fish with grilled vegetables

Blackened Steak

Read Note about blackening, below, before trying this recipe.

6 (1- to 1½-inch-thick) beef steaks (12 to 14 ounces each) suitable for broiling, such as prime rib, New York strip, filet mignon, porterhouse or sirloin

¾ cup (1½ sticks) unsalted butter, melted

6 tablespoons CAJUN MAGIC Blackened Steak Magic®

Let steaks come to room temperature. Meanwhile, heat outdoor grill, if using. Heat 6 serving plates in 250°F oven.

Heat a large cast-iron skillet on stove over very high heat until it is beyond the smoking stage and you see white ash in skillet bottom, at least 10 minutes. Carefully place hot skillet on outdoor grill or butane cooker. Just before you cook it, dip each steak in melted butter, coating both sides well. Sprinkle 1 tablespoon Blackened Steak Magic evenly on both sides of each steak, pressing it into meat with your hands. Place 1 steak in hot skillet (cook only 1 steak at a time). Cook, uncovered, over very high heat until underside forms a blackened crust, 2 or 3 minutes. Turn steak over and cook until done to your liking, 2 or 3 minutes more. (If you like your steak really rare, use steaks at least 1½ to 1¾ inches thick.) Wipe any excess fat from skillet after cooking each steak. Serve piping hot on warm serving plates. *Makes 6 servings*

About Blackening Fish and Meat

Do not try this method indoors! If you don't have a restaurant-quality commercial hood vent over your stove, any blackened dish will set off your smoke alarms and will smoke you out of the house! For blackened dishes, cook outdoors on a gas grill or a butane cooker. Or you can use a charcoal grill, but you may need to make the coals hotter by giving them extra oxygen. A normal charcoal fire may not get hot enough to "blacken" the fish or meat properly. An easy way to add extra oxygen is simply to vigorously fan the coals with a piece of cardboard until they glow. Meanwhile, heat your cast-iron skillet as hot as possible on your kitchen stove, at least 10 minutes or until it is beyond the smoking stage and you see white ash in the skillet bottom. When the coals are glowing, use very thick pot holders to carefully transfer the hot skillet to the grill.

Blackened dishes are also great cooked directly in the flames on a charcoal or gas grill. When the coals are glowing, add some chunks of hickory or other hardwood to get a flame for cooking; have the flames reaching above the grates before putting on the fish or meat. As the wood burns up, continue to add more wood chunks.

Blackened Redfish

Read Note about blackening, page 8, before trying this recipe.

1 1/2 cups (3 sticks) unsalted butter, melted, in all
6 (1/2- to 3/4-inch-thick) redfish or other firm-fleshed fish fillets (8 to 10 ounces each)*
3 tablespoons plus 2 teaspoons CAJUN MAGIC Blackened Redfish Magic®

Heat outdoor grill, if using. Heat large cast-iron skillet on stove over very high heat until it is beyond the smoking stage and you see white ash in skillet bottom, at least 10 minutes.

Meanwhile, pour 2 tablespoons of the melted butter in each of 6 small ramekins; reserve and keep warm. Reserve the remaining butter. Heat 6 serving plates in 250°F oven.

Dip each fillet in the reserved melted butter so that both sides are well coated, then sprinkle Blackened Redfish Magic generously and evenly on both sides of fillets, patting it in by hand. Carefully place skillet on hot outdoor grill or butane cooker. Place 1 or 2 fillets in skillet and pour 1 teaspoon of the melted butter on top of each. (Be careful; butter may flare up.) Cook, uncovered, over very high heat until underside forms a blackened crust, about 2 minutes. (Time will vary according to fillet's thickness and heat of skillet.) Turn fish over and pour 1 teaspoon of the butter on top of each. Cook until fish is cooked through, about 2 minutes more. Repeat with remaining fillets. Serve piping hot.

To serve, place a fillet and a ramekin of melted butter on each plate.

Makes 6 servings

*Redfish and pompano are ideal for this method of cooking. If tilefish is used, you may have to split the fillets in half horizontally to have the proper thickness. If you can't get any of these fish, red snapper, walleye pike or sacalait fillets, or salmon or tuna steaks can be substituted. In any case, the fillets or steaks must not be more than 3/4 inch thick.

Big Bang Barbecue Sauce

Generously brush this sauce over the meat when it's almost finished cooking and get ready to taste the fireworks!

½ cup (1 stick) margarine
½ cup vegetable oil
5 tablespoons CAJUN MAGIC Meat Magic®, in all
5 cups chopped onions, in all
2 cups chopped celery, in all
½ cup freshly squeezed lemon juice
2 cups canned crushed tomatoes
1 cup canned tomato puree
2 tablespoons minced garlic
1¼ cups packed dark brown sugar, in all
1 tablespoon grated fresh lemon peel
½ of an unpeeled medium orange, cut into quarters
5 cups Basic Chicken Stock (page 31), or water, in all
4 bay leaves
½ cup cider vinegar

In heavy 12-inch skillet over high heat, melt margarine with oil. When it comes to a hard sizzle, stir in 4 tablespoons of the Meat Magic. Cook, stirring frequently, about 1 minute or until Meat Magic starts to darken. Add 3 cups of the onions and 1 cup of the celery. Stir well and cook about 2 minutes. Cover and cook about 3 minutes. Stir well, scraping up any browned bits from bottom of pan. Re-cover and cook 3 minutes more. Stir and scrape pan bottom well. Re-cover and cook 3½ minutes more. Stir and scrape well to get up all browned bits. Re-cover and cook about 3 minutes more. Add lemon juice to deglaze pan. Stir and scrape sides and bottom of pan well to get up all browned bits. Cook about 1 minute, stirring occasionally. Add crushed tomatoes, tomato puree, garlic, ½ cup of the brown sugar and the lemon peel. Cook about 2 minutes; add orange quarters and the remaining Meat Magic. Cook 3 minutes more, stirring occasionally. Add 2 cups of the stock, the remaining onions and celery and the bay leaves. Stir to mix well. Cook about 7 minutes, stirring occasionally. Stir in 1 cup more stock and cook, stirring occasionally, about 5 minutes or until sauce is boiling. Reduce heat to low and simmer, stirring occasionally, about 30 minutes. Stir in 1 cup more stock, the remaining brown sugar and the vinegar. Cook, stirring occasionally, about 40 minutes; stir in the remaining stock. Cook, stirring occasionally, 45 minutes or until sauce has thickened somewhat and flavors have blended.

Makes about 2 quarts

From top to bottom: Big Bang Barbecue Sauce, Honey Almond Grilling Glaze (see page 13) and Onion Molasses Barbecue Sauce (see page 13)

New American Barbecue Sauce

This sauce complements the flavor of seafood, pork, ham, beef, chicken, sausage or anything else that strikes your fancy. Brush it on during the last few minutes of cooking time and enjoy!

Seasoning Mix (recipe follows)
1 cup vegetable oil
4 tablespoons margarine
1/2 cup orange marmalade
1 cup apricot preserves
4 cups Basic Chicken Stock (page 31), or water, in all
1/2 cup freshly squeezed orange juice
2 cups chopped green bell peppers
2 tablespoons minced garlic
1 cup chopped celery
1 cup fig preserves
1 cup chopped onion
1 teaspoon CAJUN MAGIC Pork and Veal Magic®

In heavy 12-inch skillet over medium heat, toast Seasoning Mix, stirring frequently, about 3 minutes or until smoke is visible and seasonings begin to darken. Whisk in oil; cook about 1 minute more. Add margarine and as it melts, whisk until all is incorporated. Whisk in marmalade and apricot preserves. Cook about 2 minutes, whisking frequently. Whisk in 2 cups of the stock and the orange juice. Cook, whisking occasionally, about 8 minutes. Add bell peppers and garlic; cook, stirring occasionally, about 8 minutes more. Add celery and cook, stirring occasionally, about 2 minutes. Stir in fig preserves; cook, stirring occasionally, about 30 minutes. Stir in 1 cup more stock and the onion. Cook, stirring occasionally, about 5 minutes more. Remove from heat and puree half of mixture in food processor fitted with metal blade until smooth. Repeat with remaining mixture.

Return puree to skillet over medium heat. Whisk in remaining stock and the Pork and Veal Magic. Cook, stirring occasionally, about 7 minutes or until stock has cooked down and sauce is thick but still pourable and flavors have blended.

Makes about 6 cups

Seasoning Mix

3 tablespoons CAJUN MAGIC Pork and Veal Magic®
1 tablespoon ground picoso pepper*
1 1/2 teaspoons dry mustard
1 teaspoon ground ginger
1/2 teaspoon ground cardamom
1/2 teaspoon ground nutmeg
1/4 teaspoon ground cloves

In small mixing bowl, thoroughly combine all ingredients.

*Ground picoso pepper can be found in Mexican or Latin grocery stores. If you cannot find it, use an equal amount of chili powder.

Honey Almond Grilling Glaze

This glaze is wonderful on grilled seafood, chicken and pork. Brush it on right before meat is ready to come off the grill and bring some to the table for dipping.

- **11 tablespoons unsalted butter, in all**
- **2 tablespoons all-purpose flour**
- **1 cup slivered almonds**
- **2 tablespoons CAJUN MAGIC Seafood Magic®**
- **1 cup chopped celery**
- **1 cup honey**
- **1 teaspoon grated fresh lemon peel**
- **1 cup Basic Chicken Stock (page 31), or water**
- **1/8 teaspoon ground nutmeg**

In small saucepan over medium heat, melt 3 tablespoons of the butter. Whisk in flour until smooth, about 1 minute. Reserve.

In 10-inch skillet over high heat, melt remaining butter. When it comes to a hard sizzle, add almonds, Seafood Magic and celery. Cook, stirring frequently at first and constantly near end of cooking time, about 8 minutes or until almonds are browned. Stir in honey and cook, stirring frequently, about 1 minute. Stir in lemon peel and stock. Cook, stirring occasionally, about 3 minutes. Add nutmeg; cook 3 minutes, stirring occasionally. Whisk in reserved butter mixture until it is incorporated and sauce is slightly thickened, 30 to 60 seconds. Remove from heat.

Makes about 2 1/2 cups

Onion Molasses Barbecue Sauce

This sauce was created for anything that can be grilled. Just mop it on generously near the end of cooking time.

- **4 tablespoons margarine**
- **2 tablespoons walnut or vegetable oil**
- **2 tablespoons olive oil**
- **3 cups chopped onions**
- **3 tablespoons CAJUN MAGIC Poultry Magic®**
- **3/4 cup light molasses**
- **1 cup cider vinegar**
- **1/4 cup freshly squeezed orange juice**
- **1/2 teaspoon dill weed**
- **1/2 cup Basic Chicken Stock (page 31), or water**

In 10-inch skillet over high heat, melt margarine with walnut oil and olive oil. When it comes to a hard sizzle, add onions and Poultry Magic. Stir to mix well and cook, stirring frequently, about 8 minutes or until onions are browned. Stir in molasses, mixing well. Add vinegar, orange juice and dill weed. Stir well and cook about 12 minutes, stirring frequently. Stir in stock and cook about 2 minutes more for flavors to blend.

Makes about 3 cups

Blackened Hamburgers

These are great with all the traditional trimmings. Read Note about blackening, page 8, before trying this recipe.

2 tablespoons plus 2 teaspoons CAJUN MAGIC Meat Magic®
2 pounds ground beef
6 hamburger buns, optional

Thoroughly mix Meat Magic into meat. Form meat into 6 patties, each about 3/4 inch thick. Let meat come to room temperature. Meanwhile, heat outdoor grill, if using.

Heat large cast-iron skillet on stove over very high heat until it is beyond the smoking stage and you see white ash in skillet bottom, at least 10 minutes. Carefully place hot skillet on outdoor grill or butane cooker. Place meat patties in hot skillet in single layer. Cook, uncovered, over very high heat until underside blackens, 1 or 2 minutes. Turn patties over and cook until done to your liking. Wipe excess fat from skillet after cooking each batch. Repeat with remaining patties. Serve immediately as is or on hamburger buns (if desired). *Makes 6 servings*

Blackened Pork Chops or Lamb Chops

Read Note about blackening, page 8, before trying this recipe.

18 (1/2- to 3/4-inch-thick) pork chops or (1- to 1 1/2-inch-thick) lamb chops (4 to 5 ounces each)
1 cup (2 sticks) unsalted butter, melted
About 6 tablespoons CAJUN MAGIC Pork and Veal Magic®

Let chops come to room temperature. Meanwhile, heat outdoor grill, if using. Heat serving plates in 250°F oven.

Heat large cast-iron skillet on stove over very high heat until it is beyond the smoking stage and you see white ash in skillet bottom, at least 10 minutes. Carefully place hot skillet on outdoor grill or butane cooker. Just before you cook it, dip each chop in melted butter, coating both sides well. Sprinkle each side of each chop generously and evenly with Pork and Veal Magic (use between 1/4 and 1/2 teaspoon on each side), patting it in with your hands. Place chops in hot skillet in single layer. Cook, uncovered, over very high heat until underside forms a blackened crust, 2 or 3 minutes. Turn chops over and cook until done to your liking. (And don't be afraid to serve pork chops pink in the middle. Lamb chops are also wonderful served rare or medium-rare.) Wipe any excess oil from skillet after cooking each batch. Repeat with remaining chops. Serve each chop piping hot, allowing 2 or 3 chops per person.

Makes 6 to 9 servings

Blackened Hamburgers with all the trimmings

Sassy Soups & Salads

Island Chicken Salad with Brilliant Spice Dressing

1 cup Brilliant Spice Dressing (recipe follows)
3/4 pound cooked chicken, cut into small pieces
3 cups diced unpared red or green apples
2 cups diced pared pears
2 cups seedless red grapes
1 cup chopped green bell peppers
1 cup finely chopped green onion tops
1/2 cup minced celery
2 teaspoons CAJUN MAGIC Poultry Magic®

Make Brilliant Spice Dressing. Combine 1 cup dressing with remaining ingredients in large salad bowl and toss to mix well. Cover and refrigerate until ready to serve. Allow 2 cups salad per serving.

Makes 4 servings

Brilliant Spice Dressing

2 tablespoons CAJUN MAGIC Poultry Magic®
1 teaspoon ground turmeric
1 teaspoon dry mustard
1 teaspoon ground ginger
1 very ripe medium banana
1/4 cup cider vinegar
1/4 cup orange marmalade
1/4 cup mayonnaise
1/2 cup olive oil

Make a seasoning mix by thoroughly combining Poultry Magic, turmeric, mustard and ginger in a small bowl; reserve. In blender or food processor fitted with metal blade, process banana until smooth. Add vinegar, marmalade, mayonnaise and seasoning mix; process until blended. With the motor running, slowly pour in oil until oil is incorporated and dressing is thick and creamy. Cover and refrigerate until ready to use. (Use 1 cup for Island Chicken Salad. Reserve remaining dressing for another use.)

Makes about 1 2/3 cups

Island Chicken Salad with Brilliant Spice Dressing

Spicy Rice Seafood Salad

1 quart water
Juice of 1 medium lemon
4 tablespoons CAJUN MAGIC Seafood Magic®, in all
4 drum or other firm-fleshed fish fillets (6 ounces each)
1 cup canned crushed tomatoes
1/2 cup white vinegar
1/4 cup chopped dill pickle
1 cup vegetable oil
6 cups cooked rice (preferably converted)
1 cup chopped onion
1 cup chopped celery
1/2 cup chopped green bell pepper
6 large lettuce leaves

Heat water, lemon juice and 1 tablespoon of the Seafood Magic in 10-inch skillet over high heat 8 or 9 minutes or until mixture comes to a simmer. Gently lay 2 fish fillets in skillet and cook about 4 minutes or until fish changes from translucent to opaque and feels firm. With a slotted spoon, carefully remove fish and reserve. Repeat with remaining fish. Cool slightly, cover and refrigerate until thoroughly cooled.

In large mixing bowl, thoroughly combine tomatoes, the remaining Seafood Magic, the vinegar and dill pickle. Whisking constantly, slowly pour in oil until oil is incorporated and dressing is thick. Reserve.

Stir rice, onion, celery and bell pepper into dressing. Mix well. Remove cooled fish from refrigerator. Carefully break fillets into bite-size pieces and fold into salad.

To serve, line 6 serving plates with lettuce leaves. Divide salad among plates, mounding salad in center of lettuce leaves. *Makes 6 servings*

Chicken and Andouille Smoked Sausage Gumbo

1 chicken (3 to 4 pounds), cut up
2 tablespoons CAJUN MAGIC Meat Magic®, in all (see Note)
1 cup finely chopped onion
1 cup finely chopped green bell peppers
3/4 cup finely chopped celery
1 1/4 cups all-purpose flour
Vegetable oil for deep-frying
9 cups Basic Chicken Stock (page 31), or water
1/2 pound andouille smoked sausage (preferred) or any other good smoked pure pork sausage such as Polish sausage (kielbasa), cut into 1/4-inch cubes (see Note)
1 teaspoon minced garlic
Hot cooked rice (preferably converted)

Remove excess fat from chicken pieces. Sprinkle 1 tablespoon of the Meat Magic evenly over chicken pieces. Let stand at room temperature 30 minutes. Meanwhile, in medium bowl, combine onion, bell peppers and celery; reserve.

Thoroughly combine flour with remaining Meat Magic in plastic bag. Add chicken and shake until pieces are well coated. Reserve ½ cup of the seasoned flour.

In large skillet (preferably *not* a nonstick type), heat 1½ inches oil until very hot (375°F to 400°F). Fry chicken pieces (large pieces and skin side down first) until crust is brown on both sides, 5 to 8 minutes per side; drain on paper towels. Carefully pour hot oil into glass measuring cup, leaving as many of the browned bits in pan as possible. Scrape pan bottom with metal whisk to loosen any stuck bits, then return ½ cup of hot oil to pan.

Place pan over high heat. Using long-handled whisk, gradually stir in the reserved ½ cup flour to form a roux. Cook, whisking constantly, until roux is dark red-brown to black in color, 3 to 4 minutes. (Be careful not to let it scorch or splash on your skin.) Remove from heat and immediately add the reserved vegetable mixture, stirring constantly until roux stops getting darker. Return pan to low heat and cook until vegetables are soft, about 5 minutes, stirring constantly and scraping pan bottom well. Reserve.

Place stock in 5½-quart saucepan or large Dutch oven. Bring to a boil. Add roux mixture by spoonfuls to boiling stock, stirring until dissolved between additions. Add chicken pieces and return mixture to a boil, stirring and scraping pan bottom often. Reduce heat to a simmer and stir in andouille and garlic. Simmer, uncovered, until chicken is tender, 1½ to 2 hours, stirring occasionally and more often toward end of cooking time.

When gumbo is almost cooked, adjust the seasoning if desired with additional Meat Magic. Serve immediately.

For a main course, allow ¾ cup cooked rice, a piece of chicken and 1¼ cups gumbo for each serving; for an appetizer, remove meat from bones, dice and return to gumbo; allow ½ cup cooked rice and about 1 cup gumbo for each serving. *Makes 6 main-dish or 10 appetizer servings*

Note: If you substitute other sausage for the andouille, be sure to add 1 tablespoon more CAJUN MAGIC Meat Magic®.

Low-Calorie Seafood Okra Gumbo

2 dozen shucked oysters in their liquor
2 cups cold water
1 tablespoon reduced-calorie margarine, in all
2 cups chopped onions, in all
1¼ ounces tasso (preferred), or lean ham, minced
1½ cups chopped green bell peppers, in all
1 cup chopped celery, in all
1 bay leaf
1 tablespoon plus 2 teaspoons CAJUN MAGIC Seafood Magic®, in all
10 ounces fresh okra, sliced
2 cups peeled, chopped tomatoes
1 teaspoon minced garlic
⅛ teaspoon ground thyme
5 cups Basic Seafood Stock (page 31), made with shrimp shells, or water
½ teaspoon salt
1 pound shelled, deveined shrimp
½ pound lump crabmeat
¼ cup minced green onion tops
3 cups hot cooked rice (preferably converted)

Combine oysters and cold water. Stir and refrigerate at least 1 hour. Strain and refrigerate oysters and oyster water until ready to use.

Melt 2 teaspoons of the margarine in heavy 5-quart saucepan over high heat. Add about 1½ cups of the onions just as soon as margarine melts. Stir well to coat pieces. Cook, stirring occasionally, about 5 minutes or until onions start to turn brown. At that point, add the remaining margarine, the tasso, 1 cup of the bell peppers, ¾ cup of the celery and the bay leaf. Stir well and reduce heat to medium. Cook, stirring occasionally, about 20 minutes.

Add 2 teaspoons of the Seafood Magic and the remaining onions, bell peppers and celery. Cook about 3 minutes, stirring frequently. Add the okra and cook about 5 minutes more, stirring frequently and scraping pan bottom. Add tomatoes, garlic and thyme and stir well. Cook about 10 minutes, stirring occasionally.

Add stock, oyster water, the remaining Seafood Magic and the salt. Stir well. Bring to a rolling boil, then reduce heat to low and simmer about 45 minutes, stirring occasionally.

Return to a boil and add shrimp and oysters. Cook until shrimp plump and turn pink, about 3 minutes. Gently stir in crabmeat so as not to break up pieces; stir in green onions. Serve immediately with ½ cup of hot rice per serving.

Makes 6 servings

Low-Calorie Seafood Okra Gumbo

Confetti Chicken Salad

- 1/4 cup white vinegar
- 3 tablespoons CAJUN MAGIC Poultry Magic®
- 1 teaspoon ground allspice
- 1/2 teaspoon ground bay leaf
- 1/2 teaspoon salt
- 1 cup vegetable oil
- 4 cups cooked rice (preferably converted)
- 3/4 pound cooked chicken, cut into bite-size pieces
- 2 cups small broccoli flowerets
- 2 cups chopped tomatoes
- 1 cup grated carrots
- 1/2 cup chopped onion
- 1/2 cup chopped celery
- 6 large lettuce leaves

Make dressing by combining vinegar, Poultry Magic, allspice, bay leaf and salt in blender or food processor fitted with metal blade. Process until well mixed. With the motor running, slowly pour in oil until oil is incorporated and dressing is thick and creamy.

Combine remaining ingredients except lettuce in a large mixing bowl. Mix well. Stir in dressing.

To serve, line 6 serving plates with lettuce leaves. Divide salad among plates, mounding salad in center of lettuce leaves. *Makes 6 servings*

Golden Carrot Soup

- 3 tablespoons margarine
- 4 tablespoons unsalted butter
- 3 1/2 cups shredded carrots, in all
- 1 cup grated onion
- 1 tablespoon CAJUN MAGIC Vegetable Magic®, in all
- 3 cups Basic Chicken Stock (page 31), or water, in all
- 1 quart heavy cream, in all
- 1/4 teaspoon salt

In 5-quart saucepan over medium-high heat, melt margarine and butter. When they come to a hard sizzle, add 3 cups of the carrots, the onion and 2 teaspoons of the Vegetable Magic; stir well. Cook, stirring and scraping frequently, about 20 minutes. Let mixture stick slightly, but not brown. Stir in 2 cups of the stock and scrape bottom and sides of pan until clean. Cook about 5 minutes, stirring occasionally. Pour in the remaining stock and cook, stirring occasionally, about 5 minutes more or until mixture comes to a rolling boil. Whisk in 2 cups of the cream and cook, whisking occasionally, about 7 minutes. Stir in remaining carrots, cream, Vegetable Magic and the salt. Cook 16 or 17 minutes, whisking occasionally, or until soup has thickened enough to coat a spoon.

Allow soup to set 10 to 15 minutes before serving for flavors to blend.
Makes about 6 cups

Confetti Chicken Salad

Fried-Chicken Salad

We've given you a tossed salad recipe here, but you may prefer to serve this chicken in your own favorite tossed salad.

1 cup Green Onion Salad Dressing (recipe follows)
2 tablespoons plus 1/2 teaspoon CAJUN MAGIC Poultry Magic®, in all
3/4 teaspoon filé powder, optional
1 pound boneless chicken, cut into bite-size pieces
3 cups all-purpose flour
2 large eggs, beaten
1 cup milk
Vegetable oil for deep-frying
1/2 cup (1 stick) unsalted butter
1/4 cup minced fresh parsley
2 teaspoons minced garlic
2 quarts torn iceberg lettuce leaves
1 cup julienned zucchini
1 cup chopped celery
1 cup chopped green bell peppers
1 cup chopped red cabbage
1 cup shredded carrots
4 large romaine or iceberg lettuce leaves
4 to 8 tomato wedges for garnish

Make Green Onion Salad Dressing and refrigerate. Thoroughly combine Poultry Magic and filé powder (if desired). Add 2 teaspoons of the Poultry Magic mixture to chicken in medium bowl and stir until well coated. Mix flour with remaining Poultry Magic mixture in large bowl, mixing well. In medium bowl, beat eggs and milk until blended.

In large skillet or deep-fryer, heat 3/4 inch oil to 350°F. Meanwhile, thoroughly coat chicken with seasoned flour. Then drop chicken pieces, one at a time, into milk mixture and let soak together a couple of minutes. Drain; then coat chicken again with the flour, separating pieces and coating well. Carefully drop pieces of chicken into hot oil and fry until golden brown and very crispy, about 1 1/2 to 2 1/2 minutes per side. Drain on paper towels, then place in single layer in large pan. Reserve.

In skillet, melt butter over high heat; cook until bubbles are brown. Immediately stir in parsley and garlic. Remove from heat and while still frothy, drizzle over chicken; toss with spoon until coated. Reserve.

Toss together torn lettuce, zucchini, celery, bell peppers, red cabbage and carrots in very large bowl. Stir in chicken, then stir in salad dressing. Serve in 4 individual bowls lined with large lettuce leaf and garnished with 1 or 2 tomato wedges. Allow about 4 cups salad per person.

Makes 4 main-course servings for lunch or brunch

Green Onion Salad Dressing

1 large egg plus 1 egg yolk
1 cup plus 2 tablespoons vegetable oil
Scant 1/2 cup finely chopped green onions
1 1/2 tablespoons Creole mustard or brown mustard
1 tablespoon white vinegar
3/8 teaspoon CAJUN MAGIC Vegetable Magic®

Blend the egg and egg yolk in a blender or food processor fitted with metal blade until frothy, about 2 minutes. With the motor running, slowly pour in oil until oil is incorporated and dressing is thick and creamy. Add the remaining ingredients and blend thoroughly. Refrigerate until ready to use. (Use 1 cup for Fried-Chicken Salad. Reserve remaining dressing for another use.) *Makes about 1½ cups*

Beef Salad l'Orange

- 2 tablespoons plus 2 teaspoons CAJUN MAGIC Meat Magic®, in all
- 2 tablespoons white vinegar
- ½ cup chopped onion
- 1 teaspoon minced garlic
- 1 pound beef tenderloin or other tender cut, cut into narrow strips
- 1 cup dairy sour cream
- ½ cup mayonnaise
- 2 tablespoons orange marmalade
- 2 teaspoons prepared horseradish
- 1 teaspoon Creole mustard or brown mustard
- 2 quarts iceberg lettuce, torn into bite-size pieces
- 1 cup chopped zucchini
- 1 cup chopped yellow squash
- 1 cup chopped green bell peppers
- 1 cup chopped celery
- 1 cup chopped carrot

In medium mixing bowl, make paste with 2 tablespoons of the Meat Magic and vinegar. Stir in onion and garlic and mix well. Add beef strips and mix well with your hands to evenly coat. Transfer to plastic bag, seal and refrigerate overnight.

Remove beef strips from refrigerator and let come to room temperature while you make the dressing. Preheat broiler.

In small mixing bowl, make the dressing by thoroughly combining sour cream, mayonnaise, orange marmalade, horseradish, mustard and the remaining Meat Magic. Reserve.

Place seasoned beef strips in a single layer in broiler pan. Broil about 6 minutes or until well browned; turn strips. Broil about 3 minutes or until well browned. Remove from broiler and set aside.

To serve, place a bed of lettuce on each of 4 serving plates. Add chopped vegetables and beef strips and top with a generous amount of dressing.
Makes 4 servings

Dogwood Blossom Soup

1/2 cup (1 stick) unsalted butter
4 cups minced cauliflower (about 1 pound)
2 cups chopped onions
1 tablespoon CAJUN MAGIC Vegetable Magic®
4 cups Basic Chicken Stock (page 31), or water, in all
6 ounces ham, minced
2 bay leaves
1/4 teaspoon ground nutmeg
1 quart heavy cream, in all
6 cups very small caulifloweretss (no larger than 1/2 inch)

In 5-quart saucepan over medium-high heat, melt butter. When butter comes to a hard sizzle, stir in minced cauliflower and onions. Cook about 14 minutes, stirring occasionally. Let mixture stick slightly but not brown. Stir in Vegetable Magic and cook 13 minutes more, stirring occasionally and more frequently toward end of cooking time, again taking care not to let mixture brown. Stir in 2 cups of the stock and cook about 10 minutes, stirring occasionally. Add ham, bay leaves and nutmeg. Stir well and cook about 5 minutes. Add the remaining stock, stir well and cook 7 minutes more or until mixture comes to a rolling boil. Whisk in 2 cups of the cream and cook, whisking occasionally, about 8 minutes or until cream has reduced and thickened somewhat. Whisk in the remaining cream and cook, whisking frequently, about 12 minutes or until soup has reduced and thickened enough to coat a spoon. Add caulifloweretss and cook, whisking frequently, 10 minutes or until soup comes to a boil. Reduce heat to low and cook, whisking occasionally, 10 minutes more or until caulifloweretss are tender yet still firm.

Let soup set 10 to 15 minutes before serving for flavors to blend.

Makes about 10 cups

Summer Picnic Salad

1 pound cooked ham, chopped
4 large hard-cooked eggs, chopped
1 cup mayonnaise
1/2 cup chopped onion
1/2 cup chopped celery
1/2 cup chopped green bell pepper
2 teaspoons CAJUN MAGIC Meat Magic®
Shredded lettuce
Tomato wedges for garnish

Thoroughly combine all ingredients except lettuce and tomatoes in large mixing bowl. Cover and refrigerate until ready to serve.

Divide into 4 portions and serve each on bed of shredded lettuce and garnish with tomato wedges.

Makes 4 servings

Dogwood Blossom Soup

Shrimp Cankton Salad

2½ pounds medium shrimp with shells and heads
2 cups shredded purple cabbage
2 cups shredded green cabbage
½ cup minced onion
½ cup minced celery
1½ cups Green Onion Salad Dressing (page 24)
2 tablespoons plus 2 teaspoons CAJUN MAGIC Seafood Magic®
4 large romaine or iceberg lettuce leaves
4 to 8 tomato wedges for garnish

In large stockpot, bring 4 quarts water to a rolling boil over high heat. Add shrimp. Shrimp will almost immediately turn pink. Let water return to a boil (use a wooden spoon to gently stir shrimp to let water reheat more quickly), then immediately remove pot from heat and use tongs to remove one shrimp. Test for doneness by shelling and eating—this is lagniappe! (Do not overcook. The shrimp are almost ready to eat when they first turn that lovely pink color and are opaque.) If shrimp are not cooked, return pan to high heat and cook a few seconds more, just until done. Immediately pour them into a colander (reserve liquid to use as shrimp or seafood stock in other recipes) and run cold water over shrimp or place a few ice cubes on them to cool them for shelling. Shell and devein shrimp and reserve.

In large bowl, combine the shrimp, purple and green cabbages, onion, celery, Green Onion Salad Dressing and Seafood Magic. Refrigerate until chilled. Stir well, then serve on individual salad plates lined with a large lettuce leaf and garnished with 1 or 2 tomato wedges. Allow about 1 cup for a main-course serving.

Makes 4 main-course servings for lunch or brunch

Magic Sea Shell Salad

2 cups uncooked dry shell macaroni, cooked al dente according to package directions
2 cans (9¼ ounces each) water-packed tuna, drained
6 large hard-cooked eggs, chopped
1½ cups mayonnaise
½ cup chopped onion
½ cup chopped celery
½ cup chopped green bell pepper
¼ cup chopped sweet pickle
3 tablespoons olive oil
1 tablespoon plus 1 teaspoon CAJUN MAGIC Seafood Magic®
Shredded lettuce
Tomato wedges for garnish

Thoroughly combine all ingredients except lettuce and tomatoes in large mixing bowl. Cover and refrigerate until ready to serve.

Divide into 6 portions and serve each on bed of shredded lettuce; garnish with tomato wedges.

Makes 6 servings

Shrimp Cankton Salad

Decadent Caramelized Spice Soup

8 medium acorn squash
1/2 cup (1 stick) unsalted butter
3 cups chopped onions, in all
1 tablespoon plus 1 teaspoon CAJUN MAGIC Vegetable Magic®
1 1/2 teaspoons ground cinnamon, in all
1 1/8 teaspoons ground nutmeg, in all
3/8 teaspoon ground allspice, in all
1 cup Basic Chicken Stock (page 31), or water
1/2 cup packed dark brown sugar
3 cups heavy cream
3 tablespoons granulated sugar

Preheat oven to 450°F. Halve and seed squash and place in 2 (13×9-inch) baking pans with about 2 cups water in bottom of each pan. Cover with foil and bake about 45 minutes or until fork-tender. Drain squash and set aside to cool. When cool, scoop pulp out with spoon into large bowl. Reserve 11 cups pulp and set aside.

In 5-quart saucepan over medium-high heat, melt butter. When butter reaches a hard sizzle, add 2 cups of the onions, the Vegetable Magic, 1/2 teaspoon of the cinnamon, 1 teaspoon of the nutmeg and 1/4 teaspoon of the allspice; cook, stirring occasionally, about 8 minutes or until vegetables are softened. Stir in the remaining onions and the squash, mixing well. Cover and cook about 4 minutes. Stir well, re-cover and continue cooking about 5 minutes. Stir in stock, and cook 3 minutes more. Add brown sugar; stir to dissolve well and continue cooking, stirring occasionally, about 20 minutes. Remove from heat. Transfer half of mixture to food processor fitted with metal blade and puree. Repeat with remaining half, then force all of mixture through a sieve and back into saucepan. Preheat broiler. Return saucepan to medium-high heat and stir in cream. Cook, stirring occasionally, about 7 minutes or until mixture is bubbling.

Meanwhile, in small bowl, combine granulated sugar and the remaining cinnamon, nutmeg and allspice; mix well.

When soup has cooked 7 minutes, remove from heat. Ladle about 1 cup soup into an ovenproof soup bowl and sprinkle 1/2 teaspoon sugar-spice mix over top. Place bowl under broiler 2 or 3 minutes or just until sugar is crystallized. Repeat for remaining servings. Serve immediately.

Makes about 8 servings

Basic Seafood Stock

10 to 12 cups shrimp, crawfish or crab shells or 1½ to 2 pounds fish carcasses (heads and gills removed)
2 quarts cold water or enough to cover ingredients

Place shells in stockpot or heavy saucepan and cover with cold water. Turn heat to high and bring to a boil. When liquid boils, reduce heat to low and simmer about 30 minutes.

Strain, cool and refrigerate until ready to use. Freeze for longer storage.

Makes about 1 quart

Basic Chicken Stock

1½ to 2 pounds chicken backs, necks or wings
About 2 quarts cold water or enough to cover ingredients
1 medium onion, unpeeled, quartered
1 rib celery
1 medium carrot
1 large clove garlic, unpeeled
1 cup water

In single layer in roasting pan, roast chicken in 500°F oven, turning once, 30 to 45 minutes or until very brown. Transfer browned chicken to stockpot or large heavy saucepan. Add remaining ingredients except the 1 cup water and place over high heat.

Meanwhile, place roasting pan on top of stove over high heat. Add the 1 cup of water. As it comes to a boil, scrape bottom and sides of pan until clean. Pour liquid with browned bits into stockpot.

Cook stock over high heat until it boils, then reduce heat to low. Simmer at least 4 hours, preferably 8 hours, replenishing water as needed to keep stock from reducing too much.

Strain, cool and refrigerate until ready to use or up to 3 days. Skim and discard surface fat before using. Freeze for longer storage.

Makes about 1 quart

VARIATIONS
Basic Pork Stock: Substitute 1½ to 2 pounds pork neckbones for chicken.

Basic Beef Stock: Substitute 1½ to 2 pounds beef shanks for chicken.

Note: Always start with cold water. Use enough to cover other stock ingredients. If you are short on time, simmer stock 20 to 30 minutes; the flavor will still be far better than using just water.

Marvelous Meats

Mouth-Watering Roast Pork

This pork roast is so wonderful that you'll find yourself preparing all of your pork roasts, and even fresh hams, this way (and your family and friends will request it).

4 tablespoons plus 1½ teaspoons unsalted butter
1 tablespoon plus 1½ teaspoons pork lard or chicken fat (preferred) or vegetable oil
1 cup finely chopped onion
1 cup finely chopped celery
1 cup finely chopped green bell peppers
1 tablespoon plus 1½ teaspoons minced garlic
2 tablespoons plus 1½ teaspoons CAJUN MAGIC Pork and Veal Magic®
½ teaspoon dry mustard
1 pork loin roast (4 pounds) (either boneless or bone in)

Preheat oven to 275°F. Place all ingredients except roast in large skillet. Sauté about 4 minutes over high heat, stirring occasionally. Cool.

Meanwhile, place roast in baking pan, fat side up. Make several large slits in meat with a knife, being careful not to cut through to bottom. (If you make the slices down the length rather than the width of the roast, all of the carved pieces will have some of the vegetable mixture stuffing.) Stuff pockets generously with vegetable mixture, then thoroughly rub vegetable mixture over entire roast by hand. If any of mixture is left, spread it evenly over top and a little on sides of roast. Roast, uncovered, about 3 hours (or until meat thermometer inserted in meatiest part registers 160°F), then at 425°F until dark brown on top and meat is no longer pink in center, 10 to 15 minutes. Remove from oven and let stand about 20 minutes, then slice as desired.

Makes 6 servings

Mouth-Watering Roast Pork with vegetables

Fabulous Fajitas

We've called for boneless sirloin strip steaks, but you can use 2 pounds skirt steak or London broil—just be sure to use a cut that's tender enough to broil. Skirt steak is usually about 1/4 inch thick, which is perfect; London broil is about 1/2 inch thick, so you'll need to slice it in half before cutting it into strips.

1/2 cup (1 stick) unsalted butter, melted, in all
4 cups julienned onion strips
2 cups julienned red, green or yellow bell pepper strips
4 boneless beef sirloin strip steaks (10 1/2 ounces each), trimmed and cut into julienned strips
2 tablespoons CAJUN MAGIC Meat Magic®, in all
1/2 cup freshly squeezed lime juice
Flour tortillas, warmed
Sour cream
Guacamole
Tomato salsa
Shredded lettuce

In 12-inch heavy skillet, heat 4 tablespoons of the butter over high heat; add onions and sauté until onions are clear and turning brown on the edges, about 3 minutes, stirring or shaking skillet occasionally. Add bell peppers; toss or stir to combine with onions. Sauté until onions are soft and bell peppers are still crispy, about 3 minutes more, continuing to stir or shake pan (reduce heat, if necessary, to avoid burning vegetables). Transfer vegetables to a plate to stop cooking process; set skillet aside—without wiping it—to use later for sautéing meat.

Heat several sizzle platters or a large cast-iron skillet in 400°F oven.

Meanwhile, place meat strips in large bowl and sprinkle with 1 tablespoon plus 1 teaspoon of the Meat Magic, tossing to coat well. Pour lime juice over meat and toss again. Let marinate at least 10 minutes, tossing occasionally. (After 15 minutes, meat strips will break apart when pulled between your fingers.)

Heat reserved unwiped skillet over high heat, 40 to 45 seconds; add the remaining butter (it will sizzle), then pick up meat with your fingers, let it drain slightly and add to skillet, reserving marinade. Cook about 45 seconds, turning meat frequently to coat with butter. Add reserved vegetables to meat and sauté about 15 seconds, tossing constantly to combine. Add reserved marinade, and then sprinkle the remaining Meat Magic over all; cook about 1 minute more, tossing or stirring well to combine. Remove from heat and pour onto heated sizzle platters or into heated cast-iron skillet. Serve while still sizzling.

Let everyone prepare his/her own serving or plate using the traditional condiments.

Makes 6 extremely generous servings

Fabulous Fajitas

Steak Etouffée

- 1 tablespoon plus 2 teaspoons CAJUN MAGIC Meat Magic®
- About 2 pounds beef round steak, cut into 4 pieces
- 1/4 cup vegetable oil
- 1/4 cup all-purpose flour
- 3 cups julienned onions
- 1 tablespoon margarine
- 1/4 cup white vinegar
- 3 cups Basic Beef Stock (page 31), or water, in all

Sprinkle Meat Magic evenly over both sides of steak pieces. Reserve.

Heat oil in 8-quart heavy saucepan over high heat, 2 1/2 to 3 minutes or until oil just starts to smoke. Coat seasoned meat with flour and cook, in a single layer, in hot oil. Cook about 5 minutes or until meat is browned. Turn meat pieces over and cook 3 or 4 minutes or until browned. Remove with a slotted spoon and reserve.

To same saucepan, add onions and margarine; stir and scrape sides and bottom of pan well to get up all browned bits. Cook, stirring frequently, about 4 minutes; add vinegar, stirring and scraping once more. Cook, stirring and scraping pan bottom well, about 3 minutes. Stir in 1 cup of the stock and cook, stirring occasionally, about 2 minutes. Stir in 1 cup more stock and cook, stirring occasionally, about 5 minutes. Stir in the remaining stock and return browned meat to pan. Bring mixture to a boil, cover and reduce heat to simmer. Cook, stirring occasionally, about 1 1/2 hours or until gravy has thickened slightly and meat is fork-tender.

Makes 4 servings

Savory Slow-Roasted Beef

This roast is really unusual and exotic tasting—it's perfect for special occasions.

- 1 boneless beef rib eye roast (7 1/2 pounds)
- 3 tablespoons CAJUN MAGIC Blackened Steak Magic®
- 1 1/2 teaspoons dry mustard
- 6 tablespoons unsalted butter
- 1 1/4 cups finely chopped onions
- 1 1/4 cups finely chopped celery
- 1 1/4 cups finely chopped green bell peppers
- 2 teaspoons minced garlic

Preheat oven to 300°F. Trim fat on roast to 1/4-inch thickness. Lay roast, fat side up, in 15×11-inch roasting pan without rack. Combine Blackened Steak Magic and mustard in a small bowl.

Melt butter over medium heat in a large, heavy skillet; add Blackened Steak Magic mixture, onions, celery and bell peppers; stir to coat all vegetables well. Sauté 2 1/2 minutes, stirring occasionally. Add garlic and sauté 1 1/2 minutes more, stirring and scraping pan bottom well. Remove from heat and pour mixture into bowl to stop cooking process.

Starting at one end of roast, cut about eleven 2-inch slits (about 2 fingers wide) down length of roast to form pockets; do not cut through to bottom. Turn roast over carefully and rub bottom with about 4 rounded tablespoons of mixture. Carefully turn roast fat side up and stuff each pocket with 1 rounded tablespoon of vegetable mixture. Cover top and sides with the remaining vegetable mixture. Roast, uncovered, 1 hour 30 minutes for a true rare—a cool red center—or 1 hour 40 minutes for medium rare. Or check internal temperature with a meat thermometer after about 1 hour 15 minutes. (A true rare will register 127°F, medium rare 138°F, medium 148°F, medium well 158°F—and any temperature in excess of 165°F is considered well done.) Remove from oven and transfer roast to a cutting board or platter; let set 15 to 20 minutes. Carve and serve immediately. *Makes 10 to 12 servings*

Wonderful Meat Loaf

This meat loaf is absolutely scrumptious and will make a believer of anyone who has never liked meat loaf before. The recipe is best using both ground pork and ground beef, as the pork gives more flavor diversity. However, you can make it with only ground beef.

4 tablespoons unsalted butter
3/4 cup finely chopped onion
1/2 cup finely chopped celery
1/2 cup finely chopped green bell pepper
1/4 cup finely chopped green onions
2 tablespoons plus 1/2 teaspoon CAJUN MAGIC Meat Magic®
1 tablespoon Worcestershire sauce
2 teaspoons minced garlic
2 bay leaves
1/2 cup evaporated milk
1/2 cup ketchup
1 1/2 pounds ground beef
1/2 pound ground pork
2 large eggs, lightly beaten
1 cup very fine dry bread crumbs

Preheat oven to 350°F. Melt butter in 1-quart saucepan over medium heat. Add onion, celery, bell pepper, green onions, Meat Magic, Worcestershire sauce, garlic and bay leaves. Sauté until mixture starts sticking excessively, about 6 minutes, stirring occasionally and scraping pan bottom well. Stir in milk and ketchup. Cook about 2 minutes, stirring occasionally. Cool to room temperature. Discard bay leaves.

Place ground beef and pork in ungreased 13×9-inch baking pan. Add eggs, cooked vegetable mixture and bread crumbs. Mix by hand until thoroughly combined. In center of pan, shape mixture into loaf that is about 1 1/2 inches high, 6 inches wide and 12 inches long. Bake, uncovered, 25 minutes, then increase heat to 400°F and cook until done, about 35 minutes longer. Serve immediately. *Makes 6 servings*

Beef Italienne

- 1/4 cup olive oil
- 30 medium to large garlic cloves, peeled
- 2 cups chopped onions, in all
- 1 1/2 pounds ground beef
- 2 tablespoons plus 1 teaspoon CAJUN MAGIC Meat Magic®, in all
- 2 tablespoons all-purpose flour
- 1 can (5 1/2 ounces) unsweetened apple juice
- 2 cups canned crushed tomatoes
- 1 cup canned tomato puree
- 1 cup chopped celery
- 4 cups Basic Beef Stock (page 31), or water, in all
- 1/2 teaspoon salt
- 1 pound uncooked dry pasta, cooked al dente according to package directions

In 3 1/2-quart saucepan over high heat, heat olive oil about 3 minutes or until it just starts to smoke. Add garlic and stir to coat with oil. Cook about 2 minutes or until garlic is lightly browned. Remove garlic with slotted spoon and reserve.

Add 1 cup of the onions to saucepan and stir well. Cook, stirring frequently, about 8 minutes or until onions are caramelized. Remove onions with slotted spoon and reserve.

Add ground beef and 1 tablespoon of the Meat Magic. Cook, stirring occasionally to break up meat chunks, about 6 minutes or until meat has browned. Stir in flour and cook about 4 minutes, stirring as crust browns on bottom of skillet. Stir in apple juice to deglaze pan, stirring and scraping up browned crust. Cook another 6 minutes, stirring occasionally. Stir in crushed tomatoes, tomato puree, reserved onions and garlic, the celery and the remaining onions. Cook about 10 minutes, stirring occasionally at first, then frequently. Stir in 2 cups of the stock and the remaining Meat Magic. Cook about 5 minutes or until sauce is boiling. Reduce heat to low and cover. Cook, stirring occasionally, about 18 minutes. Stir in the remaining stock and the salt; increase heat to high. Cook, stirring occasionally, about 5 minutes or until sauce is boiling. Reduce heat to low and cook, stirring occasionally, 11 minutes. Pour sauce over hot cooked pasta.

Makes 6 servings

Beef Italienne

Tacos Suave de Carne con Salsa Roja

¾ cup vegetable oil, in all
1 tablespoon pure ground chile pepper*
1 pound ground beef
2 teaspoons ground cumin
1 tablespoon CAJUN MAGIC Seafood Magic®
1 tablespoon CAJUN MAGIC Meat Magic®
1 cup chopped onion
½ cup chopped green bell pepper
3 tablespoons corn flour or all-purpose flour
1½ cups Basic Beef Stock (page 31), or water
12 (6-inch) corn tortillas
Shredded lettuce
Chopped fresh tomatoes
Shredded Cheddar cheese

Heat ¼ cup of the oil in heavy 10-inch skillet over high heat 1 minute. Stir in chile pepper and cook 1½ minutes, stirring frequently. Add ground beef and cumin. Cook, stirring frequently, to break up meat chunks, about 2 minutes. Add Seafood Magic and Meat Magic and stir to mix well. Cook 1 minute more. Add onion and bell pepper. Cook 6 minutes, stirring occasionally, or until meat is well browned. Stir in flour. Cook, without stirring, about 2 minutes or until a brown crust forms on bottom of pan. Stir in stock to deglaze pan, stirring and scraping pan bottom well to get up all browned bits. Cook about 3 minutes or until sauce is boiling. Reduce heat to low and simmer about 8 minutes or until sauce has reduced somewhat and flavors have blended. Turn heat off.

In 8-inch skillet, heat the remaining oil over high heat about 3 minutes or until it reaches 300°F. Slide 1 tortilla into hot oil and, using tongs, immediately turn tortilla over and then immediately pull it out of pan. Tortilla should be very soft and pliable. Drain on paper towels. Repeat with the remaining tortillas. Blot any of the remaining oil with fresh paper towels.

To assemble, lay tortillas on serving plates, allowing 2 per person. Spoon ¼ cup meat mixture over half of each tortilla. Top with lettuce, tomatoes and cheese. Fold each half over filling. Serve immediately.

Makes 6 servings

*You can find pure ground chile pepper (ground dried chiles) in a Mexican or Latin grocery store. However, if you cannot find it, substitute an equal amount of chili powder.

Tacos Suave de Carne con Salsa Roja

Glenn's Cajun Magic Chili

This is best if made a day before serving.

2½ pounds boneless beef, such as lean chuck or sirloin (preferred), cut into ¼-inch cubes, or lean, coarsely ground beef
2 tablespoons CAJUN MAGIC Meat Magic®
2 tablespoons chili powder
1 tablespoon dried oregano leaves
1½ teaspoons ground cumin
1 teaspoon salt
2 cups peeled, chopped tomatoes
2 cups very finely chopped onions
4 cups Basic Beef Stock (page 31), or water, in all
2 teaspoons minced garlic
1½ teaspoons Tabasco sauce
6 whole jalapeños with stems, about 4 ounces*
1 tablespoon corn flour or all-purpose flour
2 cups cooked pinto or red beans, optional

In 4-quart saucepan, combine meat, Meat Magic, chili powder, oregano, cumin and salt; stir well. Cover pan and cook over high heat 4 minutes. Stir well, re-cover pan and cook 1 minute. Stir in tomatoes and onions, re-cover pan and cook 10 minutes, stirring occasionally and scraping pan bottom well each time. Add 2 cups of the stock, the garlic and Tabasco sauce, stirring well. Stir in jalapeños. Bring to a boil, then reduce heat to low. Simmer 1 hour, stirring and scraping pan bottom occasionally. (Stir gently so that jalapeño skins don't break open.) Skim fat from top of chili mixture. Then in small bowl, stir together flour and 2 tablespoons of the liquid from chili mixture until well blended. Add flour mixture, 1 cup of the stock and the beans (if desired) to chili mixture, stirring well. Simmer 40 minutes, stirring frequently and gently and making sure mixture doesn't scorch (the flour makes it more likely to scorch). Add the remaining stock; cook and stir 20 minutes more. Serve hot in bowls, allowing about 1½ cups per serving.

Makes 4 servings without beans or 5 servings with beans

Note: If you make this a day ahead, remove jalapeños but reserve them to add back before reheating; be brave and give 'em a try—they really add flavor to chili!

*Fresh jalapeños are preferred; if you have to use pickled ones, rinse as much vinegar from them as possible. If jalapeño skins are broken, the seeds will escape into chili, giving the dish extra heat; if you like very hot chili, break one or more of the chiles open near the beginning of cooking time.

Pork Chops With Browned Garlic Butter Sauce

It's best to use salted butter for the sauce because it will brown more easily.

12 (1/2-inch-thick) pork chops
2 tablespoons plus 1 1/4 teaspoons CAJUN MAGIC Pork and Veal Magic®, in all
1 1/4 cups all-purpose flour
Vegetable oil for frying
Browned Garlic Butter Sauce (recipe follows)

Sprinkle pork chops with Pork and Veal Magic (use a total of about 2 tablespoons), patting it in with your hands. Thoroughly combine the remaining Pork and Veal Magic with flour in a flat pan; reserve.

Heat about 1/4 inch oil in a very large skillet over medium-high heat until hot, about 2 minutes. Coat each chop with seasoned flour; shake off excess. Fry chops in hot oil until dark golden brown and cooked through, 4 or 5 minutes per side. (Change the oil if the coating bits start to burn.) Drain on paper towels. Prepare Browned Garlic Butter Sauce and serve immediately on heated plates. *Makes 6 servings*

Browned Garlic Butter Sauce

3/4 cup (1 1/2 sticks) salted butter
2 teaspoons minced garlic
1 tablespoon plus 1 teaspoon minced fresh parsley
1 tablespoon Tabasco sauce

Melt butter in 1-quart saucepan over high heat until half melted, shaking pan almost constantly. Add garlic and cook until butter is melted and foam on surface is barely browned, 2 to 3 minutes, shaking pan occasionally. Stir in parsley and Tabasco sauce and cook until sauce is lightly browned and very foamy, 1 or 2 minutes. Remove from heat and immediately drizzle over pork chops. *Makes about 2/3 cup*

Louisiana Barbecue Ribs

- 2 to 2 1/2 pounds country style ribs or baby back loin ribs
- About 3 tablespoons plus 1/2 teaspoon CAJUN MAGIC Pork and Veal Magic®, in all
- 1/2 pound sliced bacon, minced
- 1 1/2 cups chopped onions
- About 3 cups Basic Pork, Beef or Chicken Stock (page 31), or water, in all
- 1 1/2 cups bottled chili sauce
- 1 1/4 cups honey
- 3/4 cup coarsely chopped pecans, dry roasted
- 5 tablespoons orange juice (slice and save rind and pulp from 1/2 the squeezed orange)
- 2 tablespoons lemon juice (slice and save rind and pulp from 1/4 the squeezed lemon)
- 2 teaspoons minced garlic
- 1 teaspoon Tabasco sauce
- 4 tablespoons unsalted butter

Adjust rack about 6 inches from heat source; preheat broiler. If using loin ribs, cut ribs into 2-rib pieces. Place ribs in a roasting pan in single layer and sprinkle generously and evenly on both sides with Pork and Veal Magic (use a total of about 4 teaspoons), pressing it in with your fingers. Broil ribs until well browned on all sides, about 15 minutes, turning as needed. Reserve in roasting pan.

Meanwhile, in a 2-quart saucepan, fry bacon over high heat until crisp. Stir in onions, cover pan and cook until onions are dark brown but not burned, 8 to 10 minutes, stirring often. Stir in the remaining Pork and Veal Magic and cook about 1 minute more, stirring often. Remove from heat and reserve.

Place 3 cups of the stock in 4-quart saucepan; cover pan and bring stock to a boil over high heat. Add the reserved broiled ribs to stock (set aside roasting pan with drippings still in it). Re-cover saucepan; cook 10 minutes, stirring occasionally. Remove pan from heat and ladle 2 cups of the stock into roasting pan with drippings. Set aside saucepan containing ribs and any of the remaining stock. Stir drippings in roasting pan well to dissolve all browned bits. Reserve.

Return saucepan with bacon-onion mixture to high heat. Stir in chili sauce, honey, pecans, orange juice, lemon juice, orange and lemon rinds and pulp, garlic and Tabasco sauce. Then add stock-drippings mixture from roasting pan to bacon mixture and bring to a boil; reduce heat to low. Remove orange and lemon rinds. Cook, stirring, about 15 minutes more to let flavors blend. Add butter and stir until melted; remove from heat. Pour mixture in batches into blender or food processor fitted with metal blade; process just until pecans and bacon are finely chopped, 10 to 20 seconds. Add processed sauce to saucepan containing ribs. Increase heat to high and bring to a boil. Reduce heat to very low and simmer 10 minutes, stirring occasionally. If ribs are not tender, add additional stock to keep sauce at proper consistency and cook until fork-tender. Serve immediately.

Makes 4 servings

Louisiana Barbecue Ribs

Bronzed New York Strip Steak

Read Note about bronzing, page 57, before trying this recipe.

1 cup (2 sticks) unsalted butter
4 New York beef strip steaks (9 ounces each) or rib eyes, filet mignon, or any beef steak tender enough to broil, well trimmed, about 1 inch thick, well chilled
1 tablespoon plus 1 teaspoon CAJUN MAGIC Meat Magic®, in all

Heat heavy griddle or large, heavy aluminum skillet to 350°F, about 7 minutes over medium heat (1/2-inch flame) on a gas stove, about 23 minutes over medium to medium-low heat on an electric stove. Or use an electric skillet or griddle.

Melt butter in pie or cake pan. When griddle or skillet is heated, coat 1 chilled steak with warm melted butter (this is the classic technique of using cold meat or fish and warm butter—so the butter will adhere), then, with steak in your hand (don't lay it down on a surface), sprinkle both sides generously and evenly with a total of 1 teaspoon Meat Magic. Place steak on hot griddle or skillet surface, then butter and season another steak. Cook only 1 or 2 steaks at a time, buttering and seasoning each and placing on griddle before buttering and seasoning another. If you lay the buttered and/or buttered and seasoned steaks down on a plate or counter, the butter—and the seasonings as well—will adhere to the plate or counter. Cook steak 3 minutes, then turn and, if steaks are very lean, drizzle about 1 tablespoon of the melted butter down length of steak. Cook 3 minutes more for medium-rare. For medium, cook steaks 4 minutes per side. If steaks are less or more than 1 inch thick, adjust cooking time appropriately. Place each steak on a serving platter or plate (do not stack steaks); wipe griddle or skillet clean between batches and continue with the remaining steaks. Serve immediately on heated plates.

Makes 4 servings

Bronzed Pork Chops

Read Note about bronzing, page 57, before trying this recipe.

1 1/4 cups (2 1/2 sticks) unsalted butter
8 (1/2-inch-thick) center-cut pork chops (5 ounces each), well chilled
2 tablespoons plus 2 teaspoons CAJUN MAGIC Pork and Veal Magic®

Heat a heavy griddle or skillet to 350°F about 7 minutes over medium heat (1/2-inch flame) on a gas stove, about 23 minutes over medium to medium-low heat on an electric stove. Or use an electric skillet or griddle.

Melt butter in a pie or cake pan. When griddle or skillet is heated, coat 1 chilled chop with warm melted butter (this is the classic technique of using cold meat or fish and warm butter—so the butter will adhere), then, with chop in your hand (don't lay it down), sprinkle each side evenly with ½ teaspoon Pork and Veal Magic, lay chop on hot griddle or skillet surface. If you lay the buttered and/or buttered and seasoned chops down on a plate or counter, butter—and seasonings as well—will adhere to plate or counter. Continue with remaining chops. Reserve the remaining melted butter in a warm place.

Cook chops until underside of each is bronze in color, about 5 minutes. (Watch chops closely and you'll see a white line coming up the sides as the meat cooks; when the line is about one-half the thickness of the chops, the meat is ready to be turned.) Turn chops and, if chops are extra lean or look dry, drizzle about ½ tablespoon of the reserved melted butter down length of each. Cook about 5 minutes more or to desired doneness. Serve immediately on heated plates, allowing 2 chops per person.

Makes 4 servings

Magic Hamburgers

If you're in a hurry, you can omit the caramelized onions and just cook the seasoned ground beef, but you may need to cook patties 3½ minutes per side for medium-rare because the meat will be denser.

4 tablespoons unsalted butter
2 small yellow onions, coarsely chopped
2 pounds ground chuck, ground round, ground veal or very lean ground beef
2 tablespoons CAJUN MAGIC Meat Magic®, in all
6 hamburger buns or onion rolls
Shredded lettuce
Sliced tomatoes
Sliced red onion
Mayonnaise
Creole, Dijon or yellow mustard
Kosher dills

Melt butter in small skillet over medium heat. Add coarsely chopped onions and sauté until transparent. Reduce heat and cook until onions are caramelized, about 15 minutes. Reserve.

Place ground meat in large mixing bowl. Sprinkle 1 tablespoon of the Meat Magic over meat and work it in well with your hands. Then sprinkle the remaining Meat Magic over meat and mix until thoroughly incorporated. Add caramelized onions to meat mixture and combine. Form meat into 6 equal patties about ¾ inch thick.

Heat heavy griddle or large, heavy aluminum skillet to 350°F, about 7 minutes over medium heat (½-inch flame) on a gas stove, about 23 minutes over medium to medium-low heat on an electric stove. Or use an electric skillet or griddle.

Place about 4 patties (depending on griddle or skillet size) on griddle or skillet surface and cook 3 minutes. Turn and cook 3 minutes more for medium rare. For medium, cook 4 minutes per side. Place patties on serving platter, then wipe griddle or skillet surface thoroughly before cooking the remaining patties. Serve immediately with all the traditional trimmings.

Makes 6 servings

Perfect Poultry

Chicken Diane

6 ounces uncooked dry pasta
3/4 cup (1 1/2 sticks) unsalted butter, in all
1 tablespoon plus 2 teaspoons CAJUN MAGIC Poultry Magic®
3/4 pound boneless, skinless chicken breasts, cut into strips
3 cups sliced mushrooms (about 8 ounces)
1/4 cup minced green onion tops
3 tablespoons minced parsley
1 teaspoon minced garlic
1 cup Basic Chicken Stock (page 31), or water

Cook pasta according to package directions just to al dente stage. Immediately drain and rinse with hot water to wash off starch, then with cold water to stop cooking process; drain again. To prevent pasta from sticking together, pour a very small amount of oil in palm of your hand and rub through pasta.

Mash 4 tablespoons of the butter in medium bowl and combine with Poultry Magic and chicken. Heat large skillet over high heat until hot, about 4 minutes. Add chicken pieces and brown, about 2 minutes on first side and about 1 minute on the other. Add mushrooms and cook 2 minutes. Add green onions, parsley, garlic and stock. Cook 2 minutes more or until sauce is boiling rapidly. Add remaining butter (cut into pats), stirring and shaking pan to incorporate. Cook 3 minutes and add cooked pasta. Stir and shake pan to mix well. Serve immediately.

Makes 2 servings

Chicken Diane

Chicken Smothered in Roasted Garlic with Sweet Basil Red Gravy

Roasted Garlic (recipe follows)
2 cups vegetable or olive oil
1 chicken (about 3 pounds), cut into 8 pieces
2 tablespoons plus 2 teaspoons CAJUN MAGIC Poultry Magic®, in all
1 cup all-purpose flour
2 cups finely chopped onions
3 bay leaves
1 cup finely chopped green bell peppers
3½ cups peeled, chopped tomatoes
1 cup tomato sauce
3 tablespoons chopped fresh basil or 1½ teaspoons dried basil leaves
2 tablespoons light brown sugar
3 cups Basic Chicken Stock (page 31), or water
½ teaspoon salt
Hot cooked rice (preferably converted) or pasta

Make Roasted Garlic; reserve.

Heat oil in large skillet over high heat. Season chicken with 1 tablespoon of the Poultry Magic. Blend flour and 2 teaspoons of the Poultry Magic in another container. Dust chicken pieces with seasoned flour. Add chicken pieces to hot oil (large pieces and skin side down first) and brown 3 to 4 minutes on each side. When brown (chicken should not be fully cooked), remove chicken pieces from skillet and drain on paper towels. Pour off all but ¼ cup of oil. Reheat skillet and oil over high heat and add onions. Reduce heat to medium, add 2 teaspoons Poultry Magic and bay leaves; cook until onions are brown, stirring occasionally, about 5 minutes. Add bell peppers and cook 2 minutes.

Add tomatoes, increase heat to high and cook 1 minute. Stir in tomato sauce and basil and cook about 1 minute. Add Roasted Garlic and cook about 1 minute. Stir in brown sugar; cook about 3 minutes. Add remaining Poultry Magic; cook about 1 minute, then stir in the stock. Return chicken pieces to skillet and bring to a boil. Simmer, uncovered, about 25 minutes, stirring occasionally to keep from sticking. Add salt and cook about 1 minute more. Remove bay leaves before serving. Serve with rice or pasta.

Makes 4 servings

Roasted Garlic

35 unpeeled garlic cloves
Vegetable oil, if using

Method I: Submerge unpeeled garlic cloves in 350°F oil until outer leaves start to turn brown. Cool naturally and peel.

Method II: Place unpeeled garlic cloves on baking sheet or in shallow baking pan. Do not crowd. Bake in preheated 400°F oven until outer leaves are dry looking and edges start to turn brown, 12 to 15 minutes. Cool naturally and peel.

Chicken Smothered in Roasted Garlic with Sweet Basil Red Gravy

Chicken with a Twist

2 1/2 teaspoons CAJUN MAGIC Poultry Magic®, in all
4 boneless, skinless chicken breast halves (about 3 ounces each)
4 tablespoons margarine, in all
1/4 cup all-purpose flour
1 cup chopped onion
1/2 cup chopped celery
1/2 cup freshly squeezed orange juice
3 tablespoons dark brown sugar
1 tablespoon grated fresh orange peel
1 cup Basic Chicken Stock (page 31), or water
1 teaspoon cornstarch dissolved in 1 tablespoon water
Hot cooked rice (preferably converted)

Using a total of 1 1/2 teaspoons, sprinkle Poultry Magic evenly over both sides of chicken breasts.

In 10-inch skillet, melt 2 tablespoons of the margarine over high heat. When margarine comes to a hard sizzle, coat seasoned chicken pieces with flour, shake off excess flour and lay chicken in single layer in skillet. Cook about 3 minutes or until lightly browned. Turn and cook about 1 1/2 minutes more or until lightly browned. Remove chicken from skillet. Reserve.

Reduce heat to medium and add remaining margarine to skillet to deglaze pan. Stir and scrape bottom well to get up browned bits. Stir in onion, celery and the remaining Poultry Magic. Stirring and scraping frequently to keep browned bits from sticking, cook about 7 1/2 minutes or until vegetables are browned and soft.

Stir in orange juice and increase heat to high. Stir and scrape pan bottom and sides well to incorporate browned bits. Add brown sugar, orange peel and stock. Stir well. Cook about 3 minutes or until mixture is boiling. Whisk in dissolved cornstarch, whisking constantly. Cook about 1 minute and return chicken to skillet. Cover, reduce heat to low and simmer 10 minutes or until chicken is fork-tender and sauce has thickened. Serve with hot rice.

Makes 4 servings

Chicken Sauce Piquant

- 5 tablespoons CAJUN MAGIC Poultry Magic®, in all
- 1 cup all-purpose flour
- 2 chickens (2 to 3 pounds each), each cut into 8 pieces
- Vegetable oil for frying
- 1¾ cups chopped onions
- 1¾ cups chopped celery
- 1¾ cups chopped green bell peppers
- 1¾ cups peeled, chopped tomatoes
- 3 tablespoons finely chopped jalapeño pepper*
- 2 tablespoons minced garlic
- 1¾ cups canned tomato sauce
- 1 tablespoon plus 2 teaspoons Tabasco sauce
- 4 cups Basic Chicken Stock (page 31), or water
- Hot cooked rice (preferably converted)

In plastic bag, mix 1 tablespoon of the Poultry Magic into the flour. Remove excess fat from chicken pieces and sprinkle remaining Poultry Magic evenly on chicken pieces. Coat chicken with seasoned flour.

In large skillet, heat ½ inch oil to 350°F. Fry chicken (large pieces and skin side down first) until browned and crispy on both sides and meat is cooked, 5 to 8 minutes per side. Do not crowd. (Maintain temperature as close to 350°F as possible, but turn heat down if drippings start getting dark red-brown; don't let them burn.) Drain chicken on paper towels. Carefully pour hot oil from skillet into glass measuring cup, leaving as many browned bits in pan as possible; then return ¼ cup hot oil to skillet. Turn heat to high. Using spoon, loosen any browned bits stuck to pan bottom. Then add onions, celery and bell peppers; cook until browned bits are well mixed into vegetables, stirring constantly and scraping pan bottom well. Add tomatoes, jalapeño pepper and garlic; stir well and cook about 2 minutes, stirring once or twice. Add tomato sauce and cook about 3 minutes, stirring occasionally. Stir in Tabasco sauce and remove from heat.

Heat 8 serving plates in 250°F oven.

Meanwhile, place chicken pieces and stock in 5½-quart saucepan or large Dutch oven and bring to a boil. Cover, reduce heat to medium and cook 5 minutes. Then stir half of the tomato mixture into stock. Cover and simmer over low heat 5 minutes. Stir in remaining tomato mixture. Cover and simmer 8 to 10 minutes more, stirring occasionally. Remove from heat and serve immediately over rice. *Makes 8 servings*

*Fresh jalapeños are preferred; if you have to use pickled ones, rinse as much vinegar from them as possible.

Down-Home Corn and Chicken Casserole

2 chickens (2 to 3 pounds each), each cut into 10 pieces
3 tablespoons CAJUN MAGIC Poultry Magic®, in all
1/3 cup vegetable oil
8 cups fresh corn, cut off cob (about twelve 8-inch ears), in all
3 1/2 cups finely chopped onions
1 1/2 cups finely chopped green bell peppers
1 pound tomatoes, peeled, chopped
3 1/2 cups Basic Chicken Stock (page 31), or water
2 cups uncooked rice (preferably converted)

Remove excess fat from chickens; season chicken pieces with 2 tablespoons of the Poultry Magic and place in plastic bag. Seal and refrigerate overnight.

Remove chickens from refrigerator and let set at room temperature. Heat oil in an 8-quart roasting pan over high heat until it just starts to smoke, about 6 minutes. Add the 10 largest pieces of chicken (skin side down first) and brown, cooking 5 minutes on each side. Remove chicken and reheat oil about 1 minute or until oil stops sizzling. Brown remaining chicken 5 minutes on each side. Remove and keep warm.

Add half of the corn to hot oil. Scrape bottom of pan well to get up all of browned chicken bits and stir to mix well. Let corn cook, without stirring, about 6 minutes. You want it to brown and to start breaking down the starch. Add 1/2 tablespoon of the Poultry Magic and stir to incorporate. Then let mixture cook, without stirring, about 7 minutes to continue browning process. Stir in onions, bell peppers and remaining Poultry Magic. Cover with tight-fitting lid and cook about 5 minutes. Add remaining corn and the tomatoes. Stir to mix well; re-cover and cook 10 minutes. Transfer corn mixture to another pan and keep warm. Preheat oven to 400°F.

Add stock and rice to roasting pan. Bring to a boil, stirring occasionally. Layer chicken pieces on top of rice and cover chicken layer with corn mixture. Cover and bake 25 minutes.

Remove casserole from oven, but don't take lid off. Let set 10 minutes, covered, and then serve.

Makes 8 servings

Down-Home Corn and Chicken Casserole

Chicken and Pasta in Cream Sauce

1/3 pound uncooked dry spaghetti (thin)
6 tablespoons unsalted butter
1 tablespoon CAJUN MAGIC Poultry Magic®
1/2 pound diced, boneless, skinless chicken breast
1/4 cup finely chopped green onions
2 cups heavy cream or half and half

Cook spaghetti according to package directions just to al dente stage. Immediately drain and rinse with hot water to wash off starch, then with cold water to stop cooking process; drain again. To prevent pasta from sticking together, pour a very small amount of oil in palm of your hand and rub through pasta.

In large skillet, melt butter over medium heat. Add Poultry Magic and chicken; sauté about 1 minute, stirring occasionally. Add green onions and sauté 1 to 2 minutes, continuing to stir. Gradually add cream, shaking pan in back-and-forth motion or stirring, until mixture boils. Reduce heat. Simmer until sauce thickens somewhat, continuing to shake pan, 2 to 3 minutes. Add cooked spaghetti; toss and stir until spaghetti is heated through, about 2 minutes. Serve immediately.

Makes 2 main-dish or 4 side-dish servings

Variation: Substitute medium shelled, deveined shrimp for chicken. Substitute 2 teaspoons CAJUN MAGIC Seafood Magic® for Poultry Magic. Remove shrimp from skillet after sautéing about 1 minute. Return them to skillet after adding cooked spaghetti.

Bronzed Chicken Breasts

Read about the bronzing technique on the next page.

3/4 cup (1 1/2 sticks) unsalted butter
8 boneless, skinless, chicken breast halves (about 3 ounces each), about 3/4 inch thick at thickest part, well chilled
About 1 tablespoon plus 2 teaspoons CAJUN MAGIC Poultry Magic®, in all

Heat heavy griddle or large, heavy aluminum skillet to 350°F, about 7 minutes over medium heat (1/2-inch flame) on gas stove, about 23 minutes over medium to medium-low heat on an electric stove. Or use an electric skillet. Heat 4 serving plates in 250°F oven.

Melt butter in a pie or cake pan. When griddle or skillet is heated, coat one chilled chicken breast half with warm melted butter (this is the classic technique of using cold meat and warm butter—so butter will adhere). With chicken in your hand (don't lay it down on surface), sprinkle it evenly with about rounded 1/2 teaspoon Poultry Magic; lay chicken on hot griddle or skillet surface. If you lay buttered and/or buttered and seasoned chicken down on plate or counter, butter—and seasonings as well—will adhere to plate or counter. Continue this procedure for remaining chicken. Set aside remaining melted butter in warm place.

Cook chicken until underside is bronze in color, 4 to 5 minutes. (Watch and you'll see white line coming up sides as chicken cooks; when line is about one-half the thickness, chicken is ready to be turned.) Turn chicken and drizzle about 1/2 tablespoon melted butter down length of each breast. Cook until done, 4 to 5 minutes more. Serve immediately on heated plates, allowing 2 breast halves per person.

Makes 4 generous servings

Note: Bronzing is a wonderful cooking technique for meat and fish—and it's so simple. You actually roast one side of meat or fish at a time on a heavy griddle or in large, heavy aluminum skillet or electric skillet heated to 350°F. (You can purchase a surface thermometer, or pyrometer, to measure dry temperature of griddle or aluminum skillet.) If you omit butter stages, bronzing produces delicious reduced-fat meat and fish dishes. Just spray griddle or skillet surface with nonstick cooking spray just before adding meat.

Sweety Meaty Sauce for Ziti

2 tablespoons CAJUN MAGIC Poultry Magic®, in all
1 pound ground turkey
2 tablespoons olive oil
2 tablespoons margarine
1 cup chopped onion
1 cup chopped green bell peppers
2 cups canned crushed tomatoes
1 cup tomato puree
3/4 cup diced carrots
1 1/2 cups Basic Chicken Stock (page 31), or water, in all
1/2 teaspoon salt
1 tablespoon granulated sugar
1 tablespoon dark brown sugar, optional
12 ounces dry pasta, cooked al dente according to package directions

Mix 1 tablespoon plus 2 teaspoons Poultry Magic with turkey, working it in well with your hands. Reserve.

Heat 3 1/2-quart saucepan over high heat about 1 minute. Add olive oil and margarine and heat about 1 minute more or until margarine has melted and mixture comes to a hard sizzle. Add turkey. Cook, stirring occasionally and breaking up chunks, until turkey is browned, about 6 minutes. Stir in onion and bell peppers and cook 3 1/2 minutes. Add the remaining Poultry Magic, the tomatoes, tomato puree, carrots, 1/2 cup of the stock, the salt and granulated sugar and stir well. (The granulated sugar counteracts the acidity of canned tomatoes, but if you like your red gravy sweet like I do, add the brown sugar, too.) Cook, stirring occasionally, about 3 1/2 minutes or until mixture is boiling. Reduce heat to medium, cover and cook about 30 minutes, occasionally removing cover and stirring before re-covering. Stir in remaining stock. Re-cover and cook, again uncovering and stirring occasionally, about 20 minutes or until sauce has thickened and has changed from bright red to dark red in color. Remove from heat.

To serve, divide cooked pasta into 4 portions on serving plates and top each with about 1 1/4 cups sauce.

Makes 4 servings

Chicken, Andouille Smoked Sausage and Tasso Jambalaya

This dish is very spicy; if your taste buds are feeling conservative, cut the amount of CAJUN MAGIC Poultry Magic® in half.

3 tablespoons unsalted butter
1/2 pound andouille smoked sausage (preferred) or any other good smoked pure pork sausage such as Polish sausage (kielbasa), cut into 1/4-inch slices
1/2 pound tasso (preferred) or other lean smoked ham, diced
3/4 pound boneless, skinless chicken breasts, cut into bite-size pieces (about 2 cups)
2 bay leaves
2 tablespoons plus 3/4 teaspoon CAJUN MAGIC Poultry Magic®
1 cup chopped onion, in all
1 cup chopped celery, in all
1 cup chopped green bell peppers, in all
1 tablespoon minced garlic
1/2 cup tomato sauce
1 cup peeled, chopped tomatoes
2 1/2 cups Basic Chicken Stock (page 31), or water
1 1/2 cups uncooked rice (preferably converted)

Melt butter in 4-quart saucepan over high heat. Add andouille and tasso; cook until meat starts to brown, 4 to 5 minutes, stirring frequently and scraping pan bottom well. Add chicken and continue cooking until chicken is brown, 4 to 5 minutes, stirring frequently and scraping pan bottom as needed. Stir in bay leaves, Poultry Magic, and 1/2 cup each of onion, celery and bell peppers and the garlic. Cook until vegetables start to soften, 6 to 8 minutes, stirring and scraping pan bottom frequently. Stir in tomato sauce and cook about 1 minute, stirring often. Stir in remaining onion, celery and bell peppers and the tomatoes. Stir in stock and rice, mixing well. Bring mixture to a boil, stirring occasionally. Reduce heat and simmer, covered, over very low heat until rice is tender but still chewy, about 30 minutes. (If you prefer to finish this dish by baking it once stock and rice are added, transfer mixture to an ungreased 13×9×2-inch baking pan and bake, uncovered, at 350°F until rice is tender but still chewy, about 1 hour.) Stir well and remove bay leaves. Let set uncovered 5 minutes before serving.

To serve, arrange 2 heaping 1/2-cup mounds of jambalaya on each serving plate for main dish; allow heaping 1/2 cup for an appetizer.

Makes 6 main-dish servings or 12 appetizer servings

Chicken, Andouille Smoked Sausage and Tasso Jambalaya

Turkey Cutlets in Citrus Custard Sauce

8 turkey cutlets or breast slices (about 3 ounces each)
½ cup freshly squeezed orange juice
2 tablespoons freshly squeezed lemon juice
1 tablespoon plus 2½ teaspoons CAJUN MAGIC Poultry Magic®, in all
3 tablespoons vegetable oil
¼ cup all-purpose flour
2½ tablespoons unsalted butter
1 teaspoon grated fresh orange peel
¼ teaspoon grated fresh lemon peel
2 cups heavy cream, in all
2 large eggs

Lay cutlets on flat tray in single layer. Mix citrus juices and pour over cutlets. Marinate 5 minutes on each side. Blot cutlets on paper towels, patting with fresh towels to remove as much moisture as you can. Lay cutlets on another tray and evenly sprinkle ¼ teaspoon of the Poultry Magic per side of each cutlet. Pat Poultry Magic in with your hands.

Heat oil in heavy 10-inch skillet over high heat about 2 minutes. Coat 4 seasoned cutlets with flour, shake off excess and lay in single layer in hot oil. Cook about 1 minute per side, or until golden brown. Remove from skillet and keep warm. Repeat with remaining flour and cutlets.

Add butter to skillet to deglaze pan. Stir and scrape browned bits up until pan bottom is clean. Stir in orange and lemon peel, and cook about 1 minute. Whisk in 1 cup of the cream and the remaining Poultry Magic. Cook about 1 minute. Whisk in the remaining cream. Cook, whisking constantly, about 2½ minutes or just until small bubbles begin forming around skillet edges. Remove skillet from heat and place on nonslip surface. (If you don't have one, wet a dish towel with hot water, wring it out, and place under skillet.)

In small mixing bowl placed on nonslip surface, whip eggs until frothy. Whisking eggs constantly, spoon a total of 4 large serving spoonfuls, one at a time, of cream mixture into eggs. Then, holding egg-mixture bowl in one hand while constantly whisking contents of skillet with other hand, slowly stream egg-cream mixture into skillet, still on nonslip surface. Continue to whisk about 3 minutes or until sauce is thick but still pourable.

To serve, ladle about ½ cup custard sauce on each serving plate, and arrange 2 cutlets in center. Serve immediately. *Makes 4 servings*

Turkey Cutlets in Citrus Custard Sauce

Succulent Southern Fried Chicken

1 chicken (about 3 pounds)
2 tablespoons plus 2 teaspoons CAJUN MAGIC Poultry Magic®
2 cups all-purpose flour
2 large eggs
2 cups milk
Vegetable oil for deep-frying

Remove excess fat from chicken and cut into 8 pieces (cut breast in half). Season with Poultry Magic and pat it to evenly distribute. Place in plastic bag. Seal and refrigerate overnight.

Remove chicken from refrigerator and let it set at room temperature. Measure flour into flat pan and reserve. Beat eggs thoroughly; mix with milk and reserve. Pour oil into large, heavy skillet.

Heat oil over high heat to 375°F. This will take about 13 minutes. When oil is hot, and not before, coat half of chicken pieces with flour. Shake off excess and drop into egg wash. Coat chicken pieces with flour again; shake off excess and place in single layer in hot oil (large pieces and skin side down first). Adjust heat to maintain 340°F as closely as possible. Turn after about 8 minutes, or when chicken is golden brown. Continue cooking about 5 minutes more and turn again. (Second turning is to assure crispness and crunchiness.) Cook about 3 minutes more; remove pieces from skillet and drain on paper towels.

Heat oil again and repeat procedure for second batch.

Makes 6 servings

Sticky Roasted Chicken

1 tablespoon plus 1 teaspoon CAJUN MAGIC Poultry Magic®, in all
1 chicken (about 3 pounds)
½ cup carrot slices, ⅛ inch thick
1 cup chopped onion

Rub 1 tablespoon Poultry Magic on outside of chicken and sprinkle remaining Poultry Magic inside cavity. Stuff cavity with carrots and onion and pull skin flaps over cavity to cover as much of cavity opening as possible. Place seasoned chicken, breast side up, in baking pan and roast in 250°F oven. Baste with pan juices after 1½ hours of cooking and then about every half hour. Roast a total of 4 hours or until drumstick rotates easily and chicken is deep golden brown. *Makes 4 servings*

Succulent Southern Fried Chicken

Fabulous Fish & Seafood

Bronzed Trout

See Note about bronzing, page 57.

¾ cup (1½ sticks) unsalted butter
4 boneless, fresh trout fillets (4½ ounces each), or other firm-fleshed fish, about ½ inch thick at thickest part, well chilled
About 1 tablespoon plus 1 teaspoon CAJUN MAGIC Seafood Magic®

Heat heavy griddle or large, heavy aluminum skillet to 350°F, about 7 minutes over medium heat (½-inch flame) on gas stove, about 23 minutes over medium to medium-low heat on electric stove. Or use electric skillet or griddle.

Melt butter in pie or cake pan. When griddle or skillet is heated, coat 1 chilled fish fillet with warm melted butter (this is the classic technique of using cold fish or meat and warm butter—so butter will adhere), then, with fillet in your hand (don't lay it down on surface), sprinkle it evenly with about ½ teaspoon Seafood Magic per side; lay fillet skinned side down on hot griddle or skillet surface. (If you lay buttered and/or buttered and seasoned fillets down on plate or counter, butter—and seasonings as well—will adhere to plate or counter.) Continue this procedure for remaining fillets. Reserve remaining melted butter in warm place.

Cook fillets until underside of each is bronze in color, exactly 2½ minutes for ½-inch-thick fillets (watch fillets and you'll see white line coming up the sides as the fish turns from translucent to opaque; when one-half the thickness of fillets is opaque, the fish is ready to be turned). Turn fillets and drizzle about 1 tablespoon of the remaining melted butter down length of each. Cook exactly 2½ minutes more. Do not overcook; fish continues to cook after you take it off the heat. Serve immediately.

Makes 4 servings

Bronzed Trout

Crusty Hot Pan-Fried Fish

The oil for frying should be just deep enough to come up the sides of the fish but not cover the top. The fish should always be in contact with the pan bottom, so never crowd pieces of fish together; fry in batches if necessary.

1 1/2 cups all-purpose flour
About 1 tablespoon plus 1/2 teaspoon CAJUN MAGIC Seafood Magic®, in all
1 large egg, beaten
1 cup milk
6 fish fillets (4 ounces each), speckled trout or drum or your favorite fish
Vegetable oil for frying

In flat pan, combine flour and 2 teaspoons of the Seafood Magic. In separate pan, combine egg and milk until well blended. Season fillets by sprinkling about 1/4 teaspoon of the Seafood Magic on each.

Heat 6 serving plates in 250°F oven.

In large skillet, heat about 1/4 inch oil over medium heat until hot. Meanwhile, coat each fillet with seasoned flour, shake off excess and coat well with milk mixture; then, just before frying, coat fillets once more with flour, shaking off excess. Fry fillets in hot oil until golden brown, 1 to 2 minutes per side. Drain on paper towels and serve immediately on heated serving plates. *Makes 6 servings*

Shrimp in Cajun Red Gravy

1 tablespoon plus 2 teaspoons CAJUN MAGIC Seafood Magic®, in all
1 pound medium to large shelled, deveined shrimp
2 tablespoons unsalted butter
3 tablespoons olive oil
1 cup finely chopped onion
1/2 cup finely chopped green bell pepper
1/4 cup finely chopped celery
2 bay leaves
1 tablespoon minced fresh garlic
2 cups canned crushed tomatoes
1 tablespoon dark brown sugar
1 1/2 cups Basic Seafood Stock (page 31), or water
Hot cooked rice (preferably converted) or pasta

Add 2 teaspoons of the Seafood Magic to shrimp and mix well to evenly distribute seasoning. Reserve.

Melt butter in heavy 10-inch skillet over high heat. Add olive oil and heat 1 1/2 minutes or until mixture comes to a hard sizzle. Stir in onion, bell pepper, celery, the remaining Seafood Magic and the bay leaves. Cook, stirring occasionally, 5 or 6 minutes or until vegetables begin to soften. Add garlic and tomatoes and cook, stirring occasionally, about 8 minutes. Stir in brown sugar and stock. Cook, stirring occasionally, about 4 minutes or until mixture boils rapidly.

Add shrimp to red gravy and stir well. Cook about 2 minutes or just until shrimp are plump and pink. Turn heat off. Cover skillet and let set about 5 minutes for shrimp to finish cooking and flavors to blend. Serve immediately over hot cooked rice or pasta. *Makes 4 servings*

Crusty Hot Pan-Fried Fish

Velvet Shrimp

3 tablespoons unsalted butter
1/2 cup finely chopped green onion tops
1 tablespoon plus 1 teaspoon CAJUN MAGIC Seafood Magic®, in all
1/2 teaspoon minced garlic
1 pound medium to large shelled, deveined shrimp
2 cups heavy cream, in all
2 tablespoons Basic Seafood Stock (page 31), or water, optional
1 cup (4 ounces) shredded Muenster cheese
Hot cooked pasta or rice (preferably converted)

Heat 10-inch skillet over high heat about 1 minute. Add butter. When butter comes to a hard sizzle, stir in green onions and 1 tablespoon of the Seafood Magic. Cook about 1½ minutes and add garlic and shrimp. Stir to combine. Cook about 2 minutes, stirring occasionally, then add 1 cup of the cream and the remaining Seafood Magic. Stir and scrape any browned bits off sides and bottom of skillet. Cook about 1 minute and stir in remaining cream. Cook 1 minute, or just until shrimp are plump and pink. Remove shrimp with slotted spoon. Set shrimp aside.

Still over high heat, whisk cream mixture frequently as it comes to a boil, then whisk constantly. Cook, whisking, 2 or 3 minutes, then add stock (if desired) and cheese. Cook 1 minute more or until cheese has melted and is incorporated. Return shrimp to skillet. Stir to coat shrimp with sauce and remove from heat. Serve immediately over pasta or rice.

Makes 4 servings

Scallops Champignon

7 tablespoons unsalted butter, in all
1 pound bay scallops
2 teaspoons CAJUN MAGIC Seafood Magic®, in all
1/2 cup finely chopped green onion tops
2 cups sliced mushrooms
1 cup Basic Seafood Stock (page 31), or water

In 12-inch skillet over high heat, melt 4 tablespoons of the butter. When it comes to a hard sizzle, add scallops and 1½ teaspoons of the Seafood Magic. Stir to combine. Cook, stirring frequently, about 3 minutes or until scallops turn from translucent to opaque. Remove with slotted spoon and reserve.

Add green onions, mushrooms and the remaining Seafood Magic to skillet. Cook, stirring frequently, about 2 minutes. Add stock and stir and scrape pan bottom well to get up any browned bits. Cook, stirring frequently, about 2 minutes or until sauce comes to a boil. Add remaining butter, whisking it in as it melts, until all butter has melted and is incorporated and sauce is creamy, about 1½ minutes. Return scallops to skillet, stir to coat with sauce and remove from heat. Serve immediately.

Makes 4 servings

Velvet Shrimp with pasta

Shrimp Creole

3 1/2 pounds large shrimp, with shells and heads
2 1/2 cups Basic Seafood Stock, made with shrimp shells and heads (page 31), or water, in all
1/4 cup chicken fat, pork lard or beef fat, or vegetable oil
2 1/2 cups finely chopped onions, in all
1 3/4 cups finely chopped celery
1 1/2 cups finely chopped green bell peppers
4 tablespoons unsalted butter, in all
2 teaspoons minced garlic
1 bay leaf
2 tablespoons plus 2 teaspoons CAJUN MAGIC Seafood Magic®
1 1/2 teaspoons Tabasco sauce
3 cups peeled, finely chopped tomatoes
1 1/2 cups tomato sauce
2 teaspoons sugar
5 cups hot cooked rice (preferably converted)

Rinse, shell and devein shrimp; make stock from shells and heads.

Heat chicken fat over high heat in 4-quart saucepan. Add 1 cup of the onions and cook over high heat about 3 minutes, stirring frequently. Reduce heat to medium-low and cook, stirring frequently, until onions caramelize, 3 to 5 minutes. Add the remaining onions, the celery, bell peppers and 2 tablespoons of the butter. Cook over high heat until bell peppers and celery start to get tender, stirring occasionally. Add garlic, bay leaf and Seafood Magic; stir well. Add Tabasco sauce and 1/2 cup of the stock. Cook over medium heat about 5 minutes for seasonings to blend and vegetables to finish browning, stirring occasionally and scraping pan bottom well. Add tomatoes; reduce heat to low and simmer 10 minutes, stirring occasionally and scraping pan bottom. Stir in tomato sauce and simmer 5 minutes, stirring occasionally. Add the remaining stock and the sugar. Simmer 15 minutes, stirring occasionally. Add shrimp and cook just until plump and pink, 3 to 4 minutes.

To serve, spoon about 1 cup sauce over 1/2 cup rice on each serving plate.

Makes 10 servings

Shrimp Creole

Magic Fried Oysters

6 dozen medium to large shucked oysters in their liquor (about 3 pounds)
3 tablespoons CAJUN MAGIC Seafood Magic®, in all
1 cup all-purpose flour
1 cup corn flour
1 cup cornmeal
Vegetable oil for deep-frying

Place oysters and oyster liquor in large bowl. Add 2 tablespoons of the Seafood Magic to oysters, stirring well.

In medium bowl, combine flour, corn flour, cornmeal and the remaining Seafood Magic.

Heat 2 inches or more of oil in deep-fryer or large saucepan to 375°F. Just before frying each batch of oysters, drain them and then use a slotted spoon to toss them lightly and quickly in seasoned flour mixture (so oysters don't produce excess moisture, which cakes the flour); shake off excess flour and carefully slip each oyster into hot oil. Fry in single layer in batches just until crispy and golden brown, 1 to 1½ minutes; do not overcook. (Adjust heat as needed to maintain temperature at about 375°F.) Drain on paper towels. Serve as a sandwich on French bread, if desired.

Makes 6 main-dish servings

Delicious Broiled Flounder

In this recipe you're broiling the fish using an overhead heat source, which makes it technically broiling, but you're cooking it in a heated liquid, which makes it poaching. One of our best friends termed the process "broaching"—and we've forgiven him. The result is fish that retains all of its natural juices. The flounder is superb served with steamed fresh pencil-thin asparagus. And we love it on a base of creamed spinach.

2 tablespoons unsalted butter
2 tablespoons freshly squeezed lemon juice or white wine
1 tablespoon plus ½ teaspoon CAJUN MAGIC Seafood Magic®, in all
4 (½-inch-thick) flounder fillets (4¾ ounces each) or trout, redfish, red snapper, bass, sole, tilefish, drum or walleye

Position rack 5 inches from heat source and preheat broiler 10 minutes. In 13×9×2-inch baking pan, add enough water to come up one-half the thickness of the fish (¼ inch deep for ½-inch fillets); add butter, lemon juice and 1½ teaspoons of the Seafood Magic. Place baking pan under broiler 5 minutes to heat the liquid.

Meanwhile, place fillets skin side down and lightly season exposed side of each with ½ teaspoon of the Seafood Magic. Pull out broiler rack and lay fillets seasoned side up in pan (water should have begun to bubble on edges and butter and Seafood Magic should have dispersed). Broil fillets until lightly browned on top and bronzed where Seafood Magic is, exactly 5 minutes for ½-inch fillets. Remove each fillet with slotted spatula—tilt spatula slightly to drain off excess liquid—then place each fillet on heated plate and serve immediately.

Makes 4 servings

Magic Fried Oysters

Buttery Bay Scallops in Lemon Dipping Sauce

7 tablespoons unsalted butter, in all
1 pound bay scallops
2 teaspoons CAJUN MAGIC Seafood Magic®
1 teaspoon freshly squeezed lemon juice
1/2 cup Basic Chicken or Basic Seafood Stock (page 31), or water
1 tablespoon minced fresh parsley
French bread

In 12-inch skillet over medium heat, melt 4 tablespoons of the butter. When butter is just melted, remove skillet from heat. Add scallops to butter and stir to coat well. Sprinkle Seafood Magic evenly over scallops and stir to coat evenly.

Return skillet to medium-high heat and cook scallops, stirring occasionally but keeping them in a single layer, about 3 minutes or just until scallops turn from translucent to opaque. Remove scallops with a slotted spoon and reserve.

Increase heat to high. Add lemon juice and stock to skillet, whisking to thoroughly incorporate all browned bits. Cook until mixture comes to a boil, about 3 minutes. Add the remaining butter, cut into pats, and as butter melts, whisk until all butter is incorporated and sauce is smooth and creamy, about 1 minute. Stir in parsley and return scallops to skillet. Bring back to a boil and remove from heat immediately. Serve with plenty of bread for dipping.

Makes 4 servings

Magic Fried Shrimp

1 3/4 pounds medium shelled, deveined shrimp
About 2 tablespoons CAJUN MAGIC Seafood Magic®, in all
1 cup all-purpose flour
1 cup corn flour
1 cup cornmeal
1 cup milk
1 large egg, beaten
Vegetable oil for deep-frying

Sprinkle shrimp generously and evenly on both sides with about 1 tablespoon of the Seafood Magic, patting it in by hand. In medium bowl, combine remaining Seafood Magic with the flour, corn flour and cornmeal until well blended. In separate bowl, combine milk and egg, beating until well blended.

Heat 2 inches or more of oil in deep-fryer or large saucepan to 375°F. Fry shrimp in small batches as follows: just before frying each batch of shrimp, coat with flour, shake off excess flour and coat with egg mixture, then coat again with flour, shaking off excess. Carefully slip shrimp into hot oil and fry just until crisp and cooked, about 1 minute; do not overcook. (Adjust heat as needed to maintain temperature at about 375°F.) Drain on paper towels and serve immediately.

Makes 6 main-dish servings

Buttery Bay Scallops in Lemon Dipping Sauce

Saucy Seafood on Rice

It's best to use fresh seafood or fish in this recipe. The sauce is best if made only three servings at a time. If you want to make more than three servings, do so in separate batches but serve each while piping hot.

- **1 cup (2 sticks) unsalted butter, in all**
- **1/2 cup finely chopped green onion tops**
- **1 teaspoon minced garlic**
- **1 pound shelled, deveined shrimp***
- **1 tablespoon plus 1/2 teaspoon CAJUN MAGIC Seafood Magic®**
- **1 teaspoon Tabasco sauce**
- **1/2 cup Basic Seafood Stock (page 31), or water**
- **1 1/2 cups hot cooked rice (preferably converted)**

Heat 3 serving plates in 250°F oven.

Place 1/2 cup (1 stick) of the butter, the green onions and garlic in large skillet. Sauté 1 minute over high heat; turn off heat. Add shrimp, Seafood Magic and Tabasco sauce; increase heat to high and sauté about 3 minutes, stirring occasionally. Add the remaining butter, breaking it into chunks in pan, then slowly add stock while moving pan back and forth on burner. Shake pan hard enough to toss but not spill ingredients. Cook over high heat 6 minutes, shaking pan constantly. Serve immediately.

To serve, mound 1/2 cup rice in middle of each heated serving plate. Spoon 1 cup sautéed shrimp and sauce around rice. *Makes 3 servings*

*You may substitute crabmeat, crawfish or oysters or firm-fleshed fish fillets (cut into bite-size pieces), or any combination of shellfish and fish to equal 1 to 1 1/2 pounds for the shrimp.

Scrumptious Side Dishes

Dirty Rice

2 tablespoons chicken fat or vegetable oil
1/2 pound chicken gizzards, ground (see Note)
1/4 pound ground pork
2 bay leaves
2 tablespoons plus 1 teaspoon CAJUN MAGIC Poultry Magic®
1 teaspoon dry mustard
1 teaspoon ground cumin
1/2 cup finely chopped onion
1/2 cup finely chopped celery
1/2 cup finely chopped green bell pepper
2 teaspoons minced garlic
2 tablespoons unsalted butter
3/4 cup uncooked rice (preferably converted)
2 cups Basic Chicken or Pork Stock (page 31), or water
1/3 pound chicken livers, ground (see Note)

Place chicken fat, gizzards, pork and bay leaves in large heavy skillet over high heat and stir well; cook until meat is thoroughly browned, 7 to 10 minutes, stirring occasionally. Stir in Poultry Magic, mustard and cumin. Then add onion, celery, bell pepper and garlic; stir thoroughly, scraping pan bottom well. Add butter and stir until melted. Reduce heat to medium and cook 4 to 5 minutes, stirring constantly and scraping pan bottom well (if you're not using a heavy-bottomed skillet, mixture will stick a lot). Add rice and cook 3 to 4 minutes, stirring and scraping pan bottom constantly (the rice should crackle and pop and look similar to puffed rice cereal). Add stock and stir until any mixture sticking to pan bottom comes loose; cook about 4 minutes over high heat, stirring occasionally. Then stir in chicken livers, cover pan and turn heat to very low; cook about 10 minutes. Remove from heat and leave covered until rice is tender, about 10 minutes. (The rice is finished this way so as not to overcook livers and to preserve their delicate flavor.) Remove bay leaves and serve immediately.

Makes 6 side-dish servings

Note: You can ask your butcher to grind the chicken gizzards and livers for you, or grind them in a food processor fitted with a metal blade. Pulse the gizzards on/off about 10 times; pulse the livers 2 or 3 times.

Magic Baked Turnips and Tomatoes

- 10 cups cold water
- 1/2 cup sugar
- 3 pounds turnips, pared and sliced into thin wedges (about 9 cups of wedges)
- 3/4 cup (1 1/2 sticks) unsalted butter, in all
- 1 tablespoon plus 2 teaspoons CAJUN MAGIC Vegetable Magic®
- 2 cups peeled, chopped tomatoes
- 1/2 cup finely chopped green onions
- 1/4 cup finely chopped fresh parsley

Preheat oven to 350°F. In 5 1/2-quart saucepan or large Dutch oven, combine water and sugar; bring to a boil over high heat. Add turnips; cover pan and cook just until turnips are fork-tender, about 5 minutes. Drain into a colander. Run cool water over turnips, tossing them until cooled thoroughly; drain well. Spread turnips out evenly in 13×9×2-inch baking pan and set aside.

In large skillet, melt 1/2 cup of the butter over high heat. Stir in Vegetable Magic and let seasonings brown 10 to 15 seconds, stirring once or twice. Add the remaining butter, the tomatoes, green onions and parsley; stir well. Cook about 1 minute, stirring occasionally. Pour tomato mixture evenly over turnips. Bake, uncovered, just until turnips are hot, about 15 minutes. Serve immediately. *Makes 8 servings*

Seasoned Squash Medley

- 5 tablespoons unsalted butter
- 2 teaspoons CAJUN MAGIC Vegetable Magic®
- 1 cup chopped onion
- 2 cups thinly sliced zucchini
- 2 cups thinly sliced yellow squash

Melt butter in large skillet over high heat. Add Vegetable Magic and stir until well blended. Add onion and sauté until golden brown, about 5 minutes, stirring occasionally and scraping pan bottom well. Add zucchini and yellow squash and cook until crisp-tender, about 2 minutes, stirring frequently and coating all vegetable slices with butter. Serve immediately.

Makes 2 to 3 servings

Magic Baked Turnips and Tomatoes

Broccoli Basile

This is a wonderfully rich side dish or lunch main dish. It is excellent served with sliced tomatoes.

6 ounces ham, coarsely chopped (about 1 cup)
1 cup chopped onion
1 1/4 to 1 1/2 pounds broccoli
3 cups water
1 cup (2 sticks) unsalted butter, in all
1 tablespoon plus 1 teaspoon CAJUN MAGIC Vegetable Magic®
1/2 to 3/4 cup very fine dry bread crumbs, in all
2 3/4 cups heavy cream

In food processor fitted with metal blade, process ham and onion together until coarsely ground, about 10 seconds. Reserve.

Cut broccoli into 3-inch flowerets. Slice thick stems of broccoli about 1/2 inch thick to make 2 cups (use any leftover stems in another dish). Place sliced stems and water in 2-quart saucepan. Bring water to a boil and continue boiling until broccoli slices are fork-tender, about 6 minutes. Drain well, reserving 1/2 cup of cooking water. Process cooked slices in food processor fitted with metal blade until minced. Reserve. Steam broccoli flowerets until crisp-tender. Reserve.

In 2-quart saucepan (preferably *not* a nonstick type), melt 1/2 cup of the butter over high heat. Stir in ground ham and onion and cook until mixture starts to stick excessively to pan bottom, 3 to 4 minutes, stirring occasionally. (The constant buildup of browned material on pan bottom—which is fairly easy to scrape off with a spoon—is what gives flavor to the dish.) Reduce heat to medium and cook 5 minutes more, stirring occasionally and scraping pan bottom well. Add Vegetable Magic; stir well and cook 2 to 3 minutes, stirring occasionally and scraping pan bottom well. Add the reserved 1/2 cup broccoli cooking water and minced broccoli stems, stirring well; cook 10 minutes, stirring and scraping frequently. Add the remaining butter and 1/2 cup of the bread crumbs; stir well. Cook, stirring and scraping, about 3 minutes. If surface of mixture looks a little oily, add the remaining 1/4 cup bread crumbs and stir well. Add cream and stir, scraping pan bottom well; continue cooking and stirring about 4 minutes. Stir in steamed broccoli, cover pan and remove from heat; let set 10 minutes. Serve immediately.

Makes 6 to 8 side-dish servings

Wonderfully Flavored Skillet Greens

4 tablespoons margarine
2 cups chopped onions
2 tablespoons CAJUN MAGIC Seafood Magic®, in all
1/2 pound smoked (preferably not water-cured) picnic ham or lean smoked ham, cut into 1/2-inch pieces
2 cups peeled, chopped tomatoes
1 teaspoon minced garlic
2 bay leaves
1 1/4 pounds cleaned and picked over mustard and/or collard greens, torn into pieces (about 12 packed cups)*
2 cups Basic Chicken Stock (page 31), or water, in all

Melt margarine in 4-quart saucepan over high heat. Add onions and sauté about 4 minutes, stirring occasionally. Add 1 tablespoon of the Seafood Magic, stirring well. Cook until onions start to brown, about 3 minutes, stirring occasionally. Add ham and cook about 2 minutes, stirring fairly often. Add tomatoes, garlic and bay leaves, stirring well; cook about 1 minute. Add greens and cook about 7 minutes, stirring occasionally. Stir in remaining Seafood Magic and cook about 2 minutes. Add 1/2 cup of the stock; reduce heat to low and simmer about 20 minutes, stirring occasionally. Add remaining stock and continue simmering until greens are tender and flavors blend, about 25 minutes more, stirring occasionally. Discard bay leaves and serve immediately.

Makes 6 servings

*You may substitute any other greens, such as spinach, for all or part of the mustard and collard greens.

Magic Broiled Tomatoes

2 medium tomatoes, peeled
1 tablespoon plus 1 teaspoon unsalted butter, softened
2 teaspoons CAJUN MAGIC Vegetable Magic®
1 tablespoon grated Parmesan cheese, optional

Score tomatoes about 4 times across top to about halfway down; reserve. Make paste of butter, Vegetable Magic and Parmesan cheese. Spread half the mixture on top of each tomato, pushing a little mixture down into the scoring. Place tomatoes in shallow pan, seasoned side up. Broil with tomato tops about 1 inch from heat until tops are brown and crusty, about 3 minutes. Serve immediately with any juices from bottom of pan spooned over top.

Makes 2 servings

Magic Onion Rings

Seasoned Flour (recipe follows)
Egg-Buttermilk Wash (recipe follows)
6 large yellow onions
2 tablespoons CAJUN MAGIC Vegetable Magic®
Vegetable or peanut oil for deep-frying

Make Seasoned Flour and Egg-Buttermilk Wash; reserve.

Peel onions and slice each onion into 3/8- to 1/2-inch rounds. Separate into rings. Lightly dust with Vegetable Magic.

In large heavy skillet or deep-fryer, heat 2 inches oil to 350°F. When oil reaches 350°F, coat onion rings with Seasoned Flour and then drop into Egg-Buttermilk Wash. Place coated rings back in Seasoned Flour to recoat and shake off excess flour. Fry in batches in hot oil, turning as needed to brown evenly, 3 or 4 minutes or until golden brown. Drain on paper towels. Serve immediately. *Makes 8 servings*

Seasoned Flour

4 cups all-purpose flour
2 tablespoons CAJUN MAGIC Vegetable Magic®
1 tablespoon salt
1 tablespoon ground white pepper
1 tablespoon ground black pepper

Combine all ingredients in medium mixing bowl, mixing well to evenly distribute seasonings. Reserve.

Egg-Buttermilk Wash

1 large egg
2 cups buttermilk
2 tablespoons CAJUN MAGIC Vegetable Magic®
1 tablespoon salt
1 tablespoon ground white pepper
1 tablespoon ground black pepper
2 1/4 teaspoons light brown sugar

In medium mixing bowl, beat egg and whisk in buttermilk. Whisk in Vegetable Magic, salt, peppers and brown sugar. Reserve.

Magic Onion Rings

Smothered Potatoes

- Vegetable oil for deep-frying
- 3 pounds russet potatoes, pared and cut into 1/4-inch-thick slices
- 1 tablespoon plus 2 teaspoons CAJUN MAGIC Meat Magic®
- 3 ounces sliced bacon, finely chopped (about 1/2 cup)
- 4 ounces ham, chopped (about 3/4 cup)
- 1 cup chopped onion
- 1 cup Basic Chicken Stock (page 31), or water
- 2 tablespoons unsalted butter

Preheat oven to 400°F. In large heavy skillet or deep fryer, heat 1 inch oil to 350°F. Add potatoes and fry in small batches until they start to brown but are not completely cooked, about 5 minutes. (Adjust heat as necessary to maintain temperature at about 350°F.) Drain on paper towels, then place potatoes in a 13×9×2-inch baking pan. Sprinkle potatoes evenly with Meat Magic and set aside.

In large skillet, fry bacon over high heat until brown. Add ham and cook 3 to 5 minutes, stirring frequently. Stir in onion and continue cooking 5 minutes, stirring occasionally. With a slotted spoon, spoon bacon mixture on top of potatoes. Add stock and butter; stir until well mixed. Bake, uncovered, until potatoes are well browned, about 35 to 40 minutes, stirring about every 10 minutes. *Makes 6 servings*

Variation: Substitute any of the other CAJUN MAGIC blends except Blackened Steak Magic for the Meat Magic.

Crisp Tender Sautéed Carrots

- 5 cups water
- 2 tablespoons sugar
- 4 cups thinly sliced carrots
- 3 tablespoons unsalted butter
- 1 cup chopped onion
- 2 1/2 teaspoons CAJUN MAGIC Vegetable Magic®

Combine water and sugar in 2-quart saucepan and bring to a boil. Add carrots and blanch 1 or 2 minutes; drain well and reserve.

Melt butter in large skillet over high heat. Add onion and sauté until brown, about 5 minutes, stirring occasionally. Add carrots and Vegetable Magic, stirring well. Reduce heat to medium and cover skillet; cook until carrots are tender but still firm, 6 to 8 minutes, stirring occasionally. Serve immediately. *Makes 4 to 6 servings*

Magic Pasta

The sauce for Magic Pasta is best if made only two serving portions at a time. If you want to make more than two servings, do so in separate batches and serve each while piping hot.

2 quarts water
1 tablespoon salt
1 tablespoon vegetable oil
1/2 pound fresh uncooked spaghetti, or 1/3 pound dry
Vegetable oil
1/2 cup (1 stick) unsalted butter, in all
1 tablespoon CAJUN MAGIC Poultry Magic®
1/2 cup finely chopped green onions
1 1/4 cups heavy cream

Place water, salt and 1 tablespoon oil in large pot over high heat; cover and bring to a boil. Add small amounts of spaghetti at a time to pot, breaking up oil patches as you drop spaghetti in. Return to boiling and cook, uncovered, until al dente (about 4 minutes if fresh, 7 minutes if dry); do not overcook.* Then immediately drain spaghetti into colander; stop cooking process by running cold water over strands. (If you used dry spaghetti, first rinse with hot water to wash off starch.) After spaghetti has cooled thoroughly, 2 or 3 minutes, pour a liberal amount of vegetable oil into your hands and toss spaghetti. Set aside still in colander. Heat 2 serving plates in 250°F oven.

In large skillet, melt 4 tablespoons of the butter over high heat. Stir in Poultry Magic and cook about 10 seconds. Add green onions; cook 1 or 2 minutes, stirring frequently. Add cream and the remaining butter; stir until butter melts. Cook about 1 minute, stirring once or twice. Add cooked spaghetti and cook just until pasta is heated through, about 1 minute, tossing constantly. Remove from heat and serve immediately.

To serve, roll half the spaghetti on large fork and lift onto each heated serving plate. Spoon half of sauce on top. *Makes 2 servings*

*Lagniappe: While cooking spaghetti, use a wooden or spaghetti spoon to lift spaghetti out of water by spoonfuls and shake strands back into boiling water. (It may be an old wives' tale but this procedure seems to enhance spaghetti's texture.)

Dressing Lissa

1 package (8½ ounces) corn bread mix
3 tablespoons unsalted butter
1 cup minced onion, in all
1 cup minced green bell peppers, in all
1 cup minced celery, in all
1 tablespoon plus 2 teaspoons CAJUN MAGIC Seafood Magic®, in all
3 tablespoons all-purpose flour
1 cup chopped (1-inch pieces) Red Delicious apple, in all
1 cup chopped (1-inch pieces) Golden Delicious apple, in all
1 cup chopped (1-inch pieces) Granny Smith apple, in all
½ cup dark raisins, in all
½ cup golden raisins, in all
2½ cups evaporated milk, in all
2 large eggs, whipped until frothy
½ pound shelled, deveined shrimp

Make corn bread according to package directions.* Reserve.

In 10-inch skillet over high heat, melt butter. Add ½ cup of the onion. Cook, stirring occasionally, 4 minutes or until beginning to brown. Stir in ½ cup of the bell peppers, ½ cup of the celery and 1 tablespoon of the Seafood Magic. Cook about 3 minutes, stirring occasionally. Add flour and stir well to evenly distribute. Cook about 3½ minutes, letting a crust form on bottom of skillet. As crust browns, stir and scrape it up to prevent burning and again let it crust, repeating procedure throughout cooking time. Add remaining onion, bell peppers, celery and Seafood Magic. Stir well. Add ½ cup each of the apples and ¼ cup each of the raisins. Cook about 5 minutes, stirring and scraping constantly. Stir in 1 cup of the evaporated milk, stirring and scraping bottom and sides of skillet until clean. Stir in remaining milk and bring to a boil, stirring occasionally. This will take about 2½ minutes. Reduce heat to simmer and cook 1½ minutes more. Remove from heat.

Preheat oven to 450°F. Coarsely crumble corn bread into mixing bowl. Pour milk mixture over corn bread. Stir to mix, but be careful not to overmix as that makes dressing heavy. Gently fold in beaten eggs. Transfer to greased 2-quart ovenproof casserole dish. Ring top of casserole with remaining apple pieces, skin side up, alternating colors. Gently push tails of shrimp into top of dressing about ⅛ inch deep in diagonal rows. Arrange remaining apple pieces in rows between shrimp, alternating colors. Sprinkle remaining raisins over all.

Cover and bake 18 minutes. Remove from oven and leave covered another 10 minutes before serving to allow flavors and juices to blend.

Makes 8 to 10 servings

*If batter does not flow from a spoon, add 3 tablespoons additional milk. If batter is not sweet, add 2 teaspoons sugar.

Dressing Lissa

Exactly Eggs

Omelette Jardinier

- **4 tablespoons unsalted butter, in all**
- **1/2 cup chopped onion**
- **1/2 pound diced cooked ham**
- **1 cup small broccoli flowerets, blanched**
- **1 cup small cauliflowerets, blanched**
- **1 cup chopped fresh tomatoes**
- **6 large eggs**
- **1/4 cup milk**
- **2 teaspoons CAJUN MAGIC Meat Magic®**

Preheat oven to 450°F. In 10-inch ovenproof skillet over medium-high heat, melt 2 tablespoons of the butter. When it comes to a hard sizzle, add onion and cook, stirring frequently, about 5 minutes or until onion starts to brown. Reduce heat to low and cook, stirring frequently, about 3 minutes more. Add ham, broccoli and cauliflower; increase heat to medium-high. Cook, stirring frequently, about 2 minutes. Stir in remaining butter to deglaze pan, stirring and scraping up browned bits from bottom and sides of pan and cook about 2 minutes. Stir in tomatoes and cook 2 minutes more.

While ham mixture is cooking, in large mixing bowl, whip eggs with milk until eggs are pale yellow and very frothy. Whip in Meat Magic.

Stir egg mixture into ham mixture. Cook about 30 seconds, or until eggs begin to set. As soon as there is a base of cooked egg on the bottom of skillet, using a spatula, pull uncooked eggs from outside of pan toward middle. This gives the uncooked egg mixture a chance to cook. Continue pulling cooked portion toward center of pan until eggs have been in skillet about 2 minutes. Place skillet on bottom rack of oven and bake about 9 minutes or until omelet is puffed and brown and center is set. Serve immediately. *Makes 4 servings*

Omelette Jardinier

Cajun Omelet

- 2 tablespoons plus 2 teaspoons unsalted butter, in all
- 2 ounces tasso or lean ham, minced (see Note)
- 1/4 cup chopped onion
- 2 teaspoons CAJUN MAGIC Meat Magic®, in all, optional (see Note)
- 6 large eggs, in all
- 1/4 cup milk

In 10-inch skillet over medium-high heat, melt 2 tablespoons of the butter. When it comes to a hard sizzle, add tasso or ham. Cook, stirring occasionally, about 1 minute. Stir in onion. Cook, stirring occasionally, about 3 minutes or until tasso and onion are browned. Remove from heat.

This recipe makes enough filling for 2 omelets, but each omelet is made individually. For the first omelet, in mixing bowl, whip 3 eggs with 2 tablespoons milk until frothy. (If using ham instead of tasso, whip 1 teaspoon of the Meat Magic into eggs and milk.)

In heavy 9-inch skillet over medium-high heat, melt 1 teaspoon butter. When butter comes to a hard sizzle, add egg mixture and cook about 30 seconds, or until eggs begin to set. As soon as there is a base of cooked egg on the bottom, using a spatula, pull eggs from outside of pan toward middle. This gives the uncooked egg mixture a chance to cook. Continue pulling cooked portion toward center of pan, cooking about 2 minutes or until eggs are cooked almost through. The top should still be a little loose. Spoon half of tasso filling over half of omelet and fold the other side over tasso to form a half-moon shape. Carefully slide omelet onto serving plate.

Repeat with the remaining butter, eggs, milk, Meat Magic (if using) and filling to make the other omelet. Serve immediately.

Makes 2 servings

Note: Tasso is a highly seasoned Cajun ham. If you use it, you won't need the Meat Magic. But if you can't find tasso, use lean ham instead and add the Meat Magic.

Andouille Smoked Sausage Puff

- 4 tablespoons unsalted butter
- 1 cup chopped onion
- 1/2 cup chopped celery
- 1/2 cup chopped green bell pepper
- 1 tablespoon CAJUN MAGIC Pork and Veal Magic® (see Note)
- 12 ounces andouille smoked sausage or kielbasa, cut into 1/4-inch rounds (see Note)
- 1/4 cup canned crushed tomatoes
- 10 large eggs
- 1/2 cup milk

Preheat oven to 450°F. In 12-inch ovenproof skillet over high heat, melt butter. When it comes to a hard sizzle, add onion, celery and bell pepper; cook, stirring occasionally, about 1 minute. Stir in Pork and Veal Magic and cook, stirring occasionally, about 4 minutes. Stir in andouille and cook about 7 minutes or until vegetables and andouille are browned. Stir in tomatoes and cook 1½ minutes more.

While andouille mixture is cooking, in large mixing bowl, whip eggs and milk until eggs are pale yellow and very frothy.

Stir beaten eggs into andouille mixture. Let cook about 30 seconds, or until eggs begin to set. As soon as there is a base of cooked egg on the bottom of skillet, using a spatula, pull eggs from outside of pan toward middle. This gives the uncooked egg mixture a chance to cook. Continue pulling cooked portion toward center of pan until eggs have been in skillet about 2 minutes. Place skillet on bottom rack of oven and bake 8 minutes or until omelet is puffed and brown and center is set. Serve immediately.

Makes 6 servings

Note: If using hot andouille sausage produced in Louisiana, use 1 teaspoon less of Pork and Veal Magic.

Red-Hot Omelet

1 tablespoon plus 2 teaspoons unsalted butter, in all
1/4 cup chopped onion
1/4 cup chopped celery
1/4 cup chopped green bell pepper
1 tablespoon plus 2 teaspoons CAJUN MAGIC Poultry Magic®, in all
2 teaspoons minced garlic
1/2 cup canned crushed tomatoes
1/2 cup Basic Chicken Stock (page 31), or water
6 large eggs, in all
1/4 cup milk, in all

In heavy 10-inch skillet over high heat, melt 1 tablespoon butter. When it comes to a hard sizzle, add onion, celery, bell pepper and 1 tablespoon Poultry Magic. Cook about 2 minutes, stirring occasionally, then stir in garlic. Reduce heat to medium and cook 2 minutes more, stirring frequently and scraping as vegetables brown and start to stick. Stir in tomatoes and cook 1 1/2 minutes more. Add stock and cook, stirring occasionally, 5 minutes more or until sauce has thickened somewhat and vegetables are soft. Remove from heat.

This recipe makes enough sauce for 2 omelets, but each omelet is made individually. For the first omelet, in mixing bowl, whip 3 eggs with 2 tablespoons milk and 1 teaspoon Poultry Magic until frothy.

In heavy 9-inch skillet over medium-high heat, melt 1 teaspoon butter. When butter comes to a hard sizzle, add egg mixture and cook about 30 seconds or until eggs begin to set. As soon as there is a base of cooked egg on the bottom, using a spatula, pull eggs from outside of pan toward middle. This gives the uncooked egg mixture a chance to cook. Continue pulling cooked portion toward center of pan, cooking about 2 minutes or until eggs are cooked almost through. The top should still be a little loose. Spoon about 1/4 cup sauce over half of omelet and fold other side over to form a half-moon shape. Carefully slide omelet onto serving plate and spoon about 1/4 cup more sauce on top.

Repeat with the remaining butter, eggs, milk, Poultry Magic and sauce to make the other omelet. Serve immediately. *Makes 2 servings*

Omelette aux Fruits de Mer

3 tablespoons plus 1 teaspoon unsalted butter, in all
1 cup chopped onion
1/2 cup chopped green bell pepper
1/4 cup chopped celery
1/2 cup minced green onion tops
1 tablespoon plus 2 teaspoons CAJUN MAGIC Seafood Magic®, in all
1/2 cup Basic Seafood Stock (page 31), or water
2 cups heavy cream, in all
1 cup sliced mushrooms
1/2 pound medium shelled, deveined shrimp
1 cup medium shucked oysters, drained and patted dry with paper towels
12 large eggs, in all
1/2 cup milk, in all

In heavy 10-inch skillet over medium-high heat, melt 2 tablespoons of the butter. When it comes to a hard sizzle, add onion, bell pepper and celery. Cook, stirring occasionally, about 7 minutes or until vegetables are softened and browned. Stir in green onions and 1 teaspoon of the Seafood Magic. Cook about 1 minute, stirring frequently. Stir in stock and increase heat to high. Cook 1 minute. Whisk in 1 cup of the cream and cook 2 minutes, whisking occasionally. Whisk in remaining cream and, whisking occasionally, cook about 6 minutes. When mixture comes to a boil, whisk constantly. Add mushrooms and, stirring constantly, cook about 1 minute. Add shrimp and cook 1 minute, stirring constantly. Add oysters and cook, stirring frequently, about 2 minutes or until shrimp are plump and pink but still firm, the edges of the oysters are curled and the sauce is thick enough to coat a spoon. Remove from heat and immediately transfer to another container to stop the cooking process.

This recipe makes enough sauce for 4 omelets, but each omelet is made individually. For the first omelet, in mixing bowl, whip 3 eggs with 2 tablespoons milk and 1 teaspoon Seafood Magic until frothy.

In heavy 9-inch skillet over medium-high heat, melt 1 teaspoon butter. When butter comes to a hard sizzle, add egg mixture and cook about 30 seconds or until eggs begin to set. As soon as there is a base of cooked egg on the bottom, using a spatula, pull eggs from outside of pan toward middle. This gives the uncooked egg mixture a chance to cook. Continue pulling cooked portion toward center of pan, cooking about 2 minutes or until eggs are cooked almost through. The top should still be a little loose. Spoon about 1/2 cup seafood sauce over half of omelet and fold other side over sauce to form a half-moon shape. Carefully slide omelet onto serving plate and spoon about 1/2 cup more sauce with seafood on top.

Repeat with the remaining butter, eggs, milk, Seafood Magic and sauce to make the other 3 omelets. Serve immediately. *Makes 4 servings*

Omelette aux Fruits de Mer

Cajun Magic Cooking Terms

Andouille Sausage—A Louisiana-produced pure pork sausage (pronounced ahn-*doo*-i). Andouille is the preferred ingredient for a number of recipes here, but if unavailable you can substitute any other good pure pork sausage, such as Polish kielbasa.

Creole Mustard—A brown mustard with mustard seeds in it—mellow, full-bodied and slightly tart. You can substitute Dijon or coarse ground mustard for Creole mustard.

Corn Flour—Corn flour is available in many health food stores and some supermarkets; it is sometimes called "fish fry." If unavailable, you can substitute all-purpose flour.

Etouffée—Literally, "smothered"; in Louisiana cooking it signifies covered with a liquid. In my family it refers to a dish with a cooked roux in the etouffée sauce. (In French Louisiana we don't put the accent on the first *e*. That would mean to smother a *person*!)

Filé Powder (Gumbo Filé)—An herb of ground young sassafras leaves often used as a flavoring and/or thickener in gumbos and other Cajun dishes.

Gumbo—A Cajun soup almost always containing a cooked roux and sometimes made with okra or filé powder. It ususally contains a variety of vegetables and meats or seafood and is served over rice.

Jambalaya—A highly seasoned rice dish strongly flavored with any combination of beef, pork, fowl, smoked sausage, ham (or tasso) or seafood (pronounced djum-buh-*lie*-ya). According to the *Acadian Dictionary* (Rita and Gabrielle Claudet, Houma, Louisiana, 1981), the word "comes from the French 'jambon' meaning ham, the African 'ya' meaning rice, and the Acadian where everything is 'à la.' "

Laginappe—A popular term in south Louisiana, laginappe means "a little something extra"—as a gift or a show of appreciation.

Roux—Traditionally, a cooked mixture of flour and oil used as a thickening agent for soups or sauces. The basic reason for using a roux is for the distinctive taste and texture it lends to food. (See Making a Roux on page 5.)

Tasso—A highly seasoned Cajun smoked ham (pronounced *tah*-so). If unavailable, you can substitute any other high-quality smoked ham, but you may need to add more CAJUN MAGIC® to the recipe for extra flavor.

Index